HOW TO **WRECK** OR **SAVE** A **CHURCH**

E D G   S M I T H

Copyright © 2023 EDG Smith.

All rights reserved. No part of this book may be used or reproduced by any means, graphic, electronic, or mechanical, including photocopying, recording, taping or by any information storage retrieval system without the written permission of the author except in the case of brief quotations embodied in critical articles and reviews.

This book is a work of non-fiction. Unless otherwise noted, the author and the publisher make no explicit guarantees as to the accuracy of the information contained in this book and in some cases, names of people and places have been altered to protect their privacy.

WestBow Press books may be ordered through booksellers or by contacting:

WestBow Press
A Division of Thomas Nelson & Zondervan
1663 Liberty Drive
Bloomington, IN 47403
www.westbowpress.com
844-714-3454

Because of the dynamic nature of the Internet, any web addresses or links contained in this book may have changed since publication and may no longer be valid. The views expressed in this work are solely those of the author and do not necessarily reflect the views of the publisher, and the publisher hereby disclaims any responsibility for them.

Any people depicted in stock imagery provided by Getty Images are models, and such images are being used for illustrative purposes only.
Certain stock imagery © Getty Images.

Interior Image Credit: Peter Johnson

ISBN: 978-1-6642-9942-9 (sc)
ISBN: 978-1-6642-9943-6 (hc)
ISBN: 978-1-6642-9944-3 (e)

Library of Congress Control Number: 2023909121

Print information available on the last page.

WestBow Press rev. date: 08/14/2023

CONTENTS

Preface xi

Chapter 1   Conditioning 1

Chapter 2   Ego 4
                     Private Agenda 7
                     Not Knowing the Congregation's Culture ... 9
                     Congregation Reduction 101 Preview 12
                         * Bay of Pigs 12
                     Congregation Reduction 101 14
                     Spring Butts 17
                     Clergy Lady 18
                     Summary 20

Chapter 3   Arrogance 22
                     General Manager 22
                     Court Martial 24
                     Performance Report 25
                     Denominational Tenets 26
                     Take This Job and Shove it 27
                     School Name Change 28
                     Steeple Chase 29
                     Summary 30

Chapter 4	Godfather Management	32
	Dictators	33
	Dump the Music Director	34
	Oh, by the Way	37
	I Don't Answer to the City!	38
	Make it Your Idea to Leave	41
	Large Memorial Service	42
	Yankee, Go Home	44
	No New Hires	45
	Summary	47
Chapter 5	Church Management	49
	Entrepreneurship	49
	Control	50
	Money to Be Spent	52
	Financial Wisdom	54
	Diocesan Rules	57
	50,000-Foot View	59
	Summary	60
Chapter 6	Church Financials	62
	Ah, Cadillac Car	62
	Pension Fund	64
	Summary	66
Chapter 7	Church Communication	67
	Candlelight Service	68
	Easter Parade	69
	Cell Phone Towers	70
	Strike While the Iron Is Hot	72
	Moving the Altar	74
	Summary	75

Chapter 8	Loyalty	77
	Leadership	78
	Music Group Is Too Large	79
	Music Loyalty	80
	Goodbye, Choir	81
	Too Many Ministries	82
	Summary	84
Chapter 9	IYI	85
	Network Engineer?	85
	Dell Computers	88
	IYI	88
	Anti-Teen	89
	Ideas	90
	Casual Destruction	91
	Too Many Ministries—Again	92
	Summary	94
Chapter 10	Job or Calling	96
	Arlington National Cemetery	97
	Stock Market	98
	Summary	100
Chapter 11	Selection	101
	Railroads	101
	Education	102
	Medicine	102
	Religion	103
	Why People Go to Church	103
	Clergy Job Description	106
	Summary	107

Chapter 12	Clear My Desk	108
	Consequences of Clear My Desk	108
	Rush to Judgment	112
	Summary	113
Chapter 13	Extrajudicialists	114
	Armed Guards	114
	Church Elders Gone Wild Preparation	116
	Church Elders Gone Wild	121
	Real Men	127
	New Church	128
	Summary	130
Chapter 14	Outside the Box	132
	The Great Baptism	132
	Root Canal	134
	Did You Enjoy Lunch?	135
	Football	136
	Congregational Melding	137
	The Great Cookie Walk	138
	Special Helper	140
	A Mass for Peace	141
	Thanksgiving Breakfast	143
	Summary	144
Chapter 15	Mysterious Ways	145
	Bible Study Surprise	145
	The House Call	146
	Sunday School Saved	147
	1984	148
	Reunion	150
	Long-Lost Friends	150

	Twelve Minutes 151
	Usher Duty.. 153
	Summary... 154
Chapter 16	Antichurch Philosophy 156
	Not This Choir... 156
	Birthday Present 159
	Not in This Church................................. 160
	Summary... 161
Chapter 17	Assorted Vignettes 163
	The Interview Ritual 163
	Assistant Clergy Interview 164
	The Great Piano Bench Fiasco................ 164
	Praise the Lord 165
	Path of a Clergy....................................... 166
	Kiddie Church... 167
Chapter 18	Summary of Lessons Learned 169
	Strive for the Perfect Clergy.................... 169
	Proactive Communication 170
	Hands-on Leadership 170
	New Church, Not a Church Redo 171
	Adequate Is Not Good Enough 172
	Ombudsman 172

Bibliography... 175

PREFACE

This book was initially conceived as a newspaper article. At a birthday party, I talked with an acquaintance, who happened to be a Baptist minister (not my denomination). After I described the article, she replied that it should be a book.

A little background about me. I'm a member of a congregation and a musician. I am not clergy, and I have not been to a seminary. As a musician, however, I have performed in a variety of churches of numerous denominations. Musicians talk about unusual actions at their houses of worship. They also talk about unusual happenings at those churches where they have played.

Following the pastor's advice, I made a list of proposed chapters and began collecting stories, anecdotes, and other tidbits that I thought would prove interesting and useful. Along the way, I decided, and I believe quite wisely, that the topics would be decided from the interviews, not from my original set of chapter headings. Not being a professional journalist, I did not engage in point-of-view journalism; rather, I let the facts and interviews drive the train.

The interviews and anecdotes collected are from all denominations—Jewish, Roman Catholic, Orthodox, and Protestant. I have obscured the denominations in order to maintain anonymity. I'll refer to the various positions and houses of worship by generic titles.

- Reverend or clergy: Title for all religious leaders. Their job description is quite simple. They have the role of a shepherd, which is to take care of their congregations, the sheep.
- Elders: Title for elders, vestry, council, session, board, etc. Their basic job description is simple. Elders should be good people with children who believe in their faith and help run the church.
- Church: An individual house of worship, church, stake, synagogue, temple, etc.
- Diocese: The regional management level of a denomination that most individual churches report to: diocese, conference, presbytery, etc.
- Bishop: The title of the religious leader at the diocesan level. Bishops are critical leaders in the overall health of the individual churches in their diocese.

※

Children have big ears that hear more than their parents think they hear. The same goes for people who participate in a religious service as clergy, staff, or as a member of the congregation; they often hear more than you think they do.

As such, I have seen and heard numerous vignettes that left individuals bewildered as they tried to understand why something occurred. These real-life encounters are the basis of this book.

I found that as I progressed in my quest for anecdotes, some individuals asked for an example. When I provided an example, some responded with "You must mean church X of denomination Y in city Z. Occasionally they identified the specific church, but usually it was a church of a different denomination in a different town.

The examples and vignettes, while based on actual events,

have (in most cases) been presented in a humorous manner and with a tad of artistic license. These vignettes provide lessons that can be learned, for the clergy, the diocese, the music directors, the staff, the church elders, and the congregants.

It is important to note that the vast majority of clergy, music directors, elders, and staff members are dedicated to their profession and/or position. They find it a calling and do not seek personal aggrandizement. Some clergy will follow the natural progression of advancement to a larger church, expansion of their church, or up to a position in the diocese. Other clergy have found their church home and will remain with an individual church for the duration of their career. Almost all clergy make mistakes as they mature in their profession. After all, like everyone else, they are human and imperfect.

A very select few will reach or exceed their level of incompetence and successfully mess things up for their entire career.

An extremely small percentage of individuals, often described in this book, view their position as a "job," have an "agenda" to implement, and have a rather unusual concept of how to run a church and how to work with people.

Now you have an opportunity to read a sampling of these events, some humorous. A few can be equated with tragedies, and possibly some you may identify with your house of worship. Some may elicit a "How could they—the clergy, elders, or staff—have made such a brilliant, or not-so-smart, decision? Don't they have any common sense?" Or "How could they—the clergy, the elders, the staff, the diocese, the bishop, the music director—have been so blind?" Or "How could the congregation have been so sheeplike, so blind, so uncaring, or maybe even so ignorant?"

Read "Conditioning" in the beginning of the next chapter. You will probably find it revealing and eye-opening.

— 1 —

CONDITIONING

A person's job title doesn't always equate to competence. We are conditioned early in life to believe that an individual's title means they are qualified to work in their field or profession. We are conditioned to believe that they have unique skills in their field or specialized niche in their profession.

Teachers are supposed to be skilled in teaching. They have a teaching credential; they have been hired by the principal, superintendent, or school board. Thus, we trust our children to their care. Teachers go to summer school for continuing education and often pay the tuition themselves.

Police have been trained to protect us from the bad guys. Additionally, they're pretty adept at reminding average people that making not-so-smart mistakes, like speeding or running a stop sign, can endanger other citizens. They make a judgment call to give a ticket or give a warning. If the citizen really makes a bad traffic mistake, they may be arrested and spend some time in the clink.

Doctors are who we go to if we have a broken leg, bad cold, or some unexplained ouchy. After all, they have been to medical school, and they have a diploma on the wall that attests to their medical knowledge and skill. We trust them. We may do research to find a doctor we believe is the one best suited for our particular ailment.

The primary reasons we go to a church are to worship, socialize, and refresh our moral compass, although a few may go for other reasons. As stewards, we give to the church in a variety of ways. Congregants serve as ushers, members of the flower guild, greeters, musicians, and so forth, in addition to giving monetarily. We usually assume that since the clergy has been ordained, they are skilled and competent in counseling, managing a church, and being the spiritual leader of the church. Hmmm!

We also assume the church staff (musicians, office staff, elders, clergy, etc.) are qualified and have the necessary skills for these positions. Another hmmm!

Ten Commandments
1. You shall have no other gods before me.
2. You shall make no idols.
3. You shall not take the name of the Lord in God in vain.
4. Keep the Sabbath day holy.
5. Honor your father and your mother.
6. You shall not murder.
7. You shall not commit adultery.
8. You shall not steal.
9. You shall not bear false witness against your neighbor.
10. You shall not covet.

After each of the following vignettes, ask yourself whether all the parties and individuals involved followed the Ten Commandments. If they had, this book couldn't have been written.

Unfortunately, there are some lousy teachers, dishonest cops, and incompetent doctors. And of course, there are some clergy and church staff who shouldn't be involved in the running of a church.

The first vignette in the next chapter, "Private Agenda," provides an interesting example of an oversized and misused ego.

— 2 —

EGO

Ego needs to be just right. A person's ego is comparable to the beds that are too soft, too hard, and just right in the fairy tale "Goldilocks and the Three Bears." Too much or too little isn't good. Just the right amount is best.

I had an interview with a senior clergy. The interview was quite different from what I had expected. The reverend stated that the clergy must have a strong ego to survive. In this situation, a strong ego is a positive trait.

The explanation was that a few members of the congregation of any church—or any organization, for that matter—often have strong opinions and desires. Those with strong opinions are usually forceful in expressing what they want. The clergy must listen and discuss their desires but do what is best for the congregation within the confines of their church's doctrine. What is good for one congregation may not be good for another.

Rick Warren, the pastor of the Saddleback megachurch in California, is also the author of several excellent books on the subject of how to run a successful church. He explained the whiner issue quite succinctly is his book *The Purpose-Driven Church*.

> You cannot let whiners set the agenda for the church. That is an abdication of leadership. Unfortunately, the smaller a church is, the more influence the most negative member has. (1995, p 92)

Beware of whiners! Whiners with big egos can steamroll a church, overriding the responsibility of the clergy. The negativity of whiners undermines the mission of the church. A whiner is unhappy with the church and wants to change it. As is often the case, they can't foresee the impact of their desired changes. When the whiner stands on their soapbox and demands that their changes be accepted, the elders and clergy must tell them to find a church they'll be happy with rather than mess up an existing church.

Some of the vignettes in this book are about whiners with big egos. The whiners believe that they are there to protect the church (their concept of the church may be different from everyone else's). Whiners don't understand, or don't want to accept, the roles of the clergy, elders, and the congregation.

If a congregant has a strong desire for a new ministry, and that ministry can be incorporated into that particular church or congregation, the task can be rather simple. However, below are some rather absurd examples:

- a new mothers' ministry in a retirement community (but it might be successful for experienced mothers in a retirement community to help new mothers outside the retirement community)
- a pro-abortion ministry in a Catholic church
- a save-the-trees ministry in a logging community
- a seminary lecture series at a homeless church

What are the factors of a successful church? I'll start with factors involved in the founding of some megachurches:

- clergy with just the right amount of strong ego
- clergy with strong self-confidence
- clergy with a strong desire to establish their church

Examples of built-from-scratch megachurches include the following:

- Adam Hamilton's Methodist Church of the Resurrection in Kansas
- Rick Warren's Saddleback Baptist church in California
- Bill Hybels's interdenominational Protestant Willow Creek Church in Illinois

Starting from zero, with strong egos (not arrogance), self-confidence, and perseverance, they created successful churches. They canvassed their communities asking what the nonchurch-attending people didn't like about churches, what they did like, and what they wanted in a church.

Bill Hybel at the Willow Creek Church identified the future congregant as Unchurched Harry. Rick Warren of the Saddleback Church identified their target congregant as Saddleback Sam. They structured their churches to accommodate the needs and desires of their congregants and the community. They did not try to sell air conditioners to Eskimos. They marketed to the needs of the community and congregation. They did not take the position of "This is my product; take it or leave it." They built the proverbial stoves, not air conditioners, for Eskimos.

Now for the first vignette, the first of many in this book that I hope you'll fine enjoyable—and perhaps eye-opening.

PRIVATE AGENDA

Rev. Al Waze Wright arrived at his new church. The reverend was thrilled with the opportunity to get things done the right way. He knew what had to be done, and how to do it. Unfortunately, Rev. Wright was an experienced (and sometimes crooked) poker player, so he held his cards very close to his vest. The staff didn't know what he wanted, nor did they notice when he slipped in a new card from his sleeve. The result was that in a year, 75 percent of the staff had departed for greener pastures.

It had been a seismic culture change. The previous reverend was focused on worship and shared the details of his goals and objectives with the staff. Rev. Wright's agenda did not include the current congregation. They could take care of themselves. He was going to build a new congregation.

Only Rev. Wright knew what he wanted, when he wanted it, and how he wanted it. His solution was to liquidate the current church program and start over. The result was the congregation was halved in two years.

Lessons Learned: One of the primary rules of management is to let your staff (your team members) know the direction you're going. They can't support you if they don't know what you want or where you're going. Somewhere along the line, the system failed several times. Rev. Al Waze Wright had a very strong ego, and I believe it was misused. He failed leadership 101.

The selection process that placed him in the church had failed. He was not a suitable fit as the leader of this particular church.

In retrospect, why didn't he add his new congregation as a new service at a different time or day? Why didn't Rev. Al Waze Wright start his ideal church from scratch? This is what Adam Hamilton and Rick Warren did, and they did so quite successfully. The result could have been two successful churches rather than one destroyed church.

NOT KNOWING THE CONGREGATION'S CULTURE

Rev. Gait Kieper was a chaplain at an overseas military installation. The congregation consisted primarily of schoolteachers and military officers. Rev. Kieper wanted everyone to be socially involved on Friday nights with the lower-ranking enlisted personnel. (Note: That doesn't work in a military structure.)

When people said, "That is not where and how we reach out," Rev. Kieper wouldn't hear them. He marched to his own drum—and apparently it wasn't a military drum.

One morning during his sermon, he announced that he had a hotline to God, and none of the congregation had such a line. Without even talking to one another, almost the entire congregation went to a local civilian church the following Sunday.

Lessons Learned: Too much ego often equals arrogance. Such a persona is rarely accepted by a congregation.

CONGREGATION REDUCTION 101 PREVIEW

I'll set the scene for the next vignette by providing some glimpses into the 1961 Bay of Pigs fiasco, as well as a staff meeting of former President Lyndon Baines Johnson (LBJ).

BAY OF PIGS

First, a little history about the Bay of Pigs. It was military invasion of Cuba undertaken by the CIA-sponsored paramilitary group called Brigade 2506 on April 17, 1961. Its goal was to overthrow the young communist-leaning government of Fidel Castro. It is important to note that President Kennedy failed to follow the detailed planning process established by his predecessor, President Eisenhower, a WW II general.

Brigade 2506 was too small, and the required United States air and naval forces in the original plan were not provided. The invasion was a failure.

Evan Thomas's book *Ike's Bluff* provides an inside look into how the Bay of Pigs became a fiasco. As you read the following excerpt, compare Rev. Mien E. Miser in the next vignette to President Kennedy.

> That morning, April 19, President Kennedy called Eisenhower in Gettysburg and asked to meet him at Camp David for a post mortem. Kennedy had never visited the presidential retreat, so, oddly, Eisenhower, the ex-president, acted as host, showing his successor around the simple cabins on the wooded Maryland mountainside. The young president was chastened, "Well, just somewhere along the line I blundered, and I don't know how badly." Kennedy told Eisenhower.

"Everyone approved—the JCS, the CIA, my staff." Eisenhower started asking a series of pointed questions to learn precisely what the military had said about the CIA plan. Uncomfortably, Kennedy admitted that the Joint Chiefs of Staff had only offered "guarded approval."

Gingerly, Eisenhower pressed a little further. "Mr. President," he addressed Kennedy, "before you approved the plan did you have everyone in front of you debating the thing so you could get the pros and cons yourself and then make a decision, or did you see these people one at a time?" Kennedy smiled ruefully and admitted that he had not forced a full or formal airing of the invasion plan. (2012, page 406)

A meeting with everyone could have resulted in following Eisenhower's plan, with or without modifications. The result would have been a successful invasion, but not the Bay of Pigs debacle.

A meeting with everyone could have resulted in following Eisenhower's plan, with or without modifications, or abandoning the entire invasion. The result could have been a successful invasion but not the Bay of Pigs debacle.

LBJ staff meeting: Years ago, I was listening to a radio program about LBJ's presidency. LBJ had asked one of his cabinet members to come back the next week with a presentation against what the member had just supported. The following week, the cabinet member presented a superb presentation against what he had supported the previous week. Later that night, the cabinet member called LBJ and said that despite his presentation against the issue, he still fully supported it. LBJ got the pros and cons of the issue involved.

CONGREGATION REDUCTION 101

The church was thriving and financially strong. It had several hundred thousand dollars in its rainy-day fund. The mortgage was paid on time, and it had a number of full-time staff and some part-time employees. The church elders had hired architects to see about increasing the size of the church building to accommodate its growing congregation.

Enter Rev. Mien E. Miser, the new senior clergy with many years of experience. He had a strong personality, gave superb sermons, and was determined to adjust this church to fit his concept of what a church should be.

This is what Rev. Mien E. Miser accomplished in two years:

* Reduced full-time staff from eight to one—just himself.
* Alienated a number of congregants by his clumsy and rude termination of longtime staff members.
* Reduced church office hours from nine to five Monday through Friday to ten to two Tuesday through Friday.
* Expanded sermon time so that there was less than five minutes between services.
* Moved beverage and snacks from the social hall to the narthex (vestibule leading to the nave/sanctuary). This successfully created a people jam for those exiting with those trying to get in.
* Created a Christmas-Time-at-the-Mall experience in the parking lot by his lengthy sermons. People waited for a parking space while those exiting waited for a traffic opening so they could back out.
* Successfully reduced Sunday attendance from seven hundred for three services to 350 for three services.
* Paid off the mortgage, thereby eliminating the rainy-day fund.

Where did the selection process go wrong, or did it go right? One former congregant theorized that the diocese wanted the church to fail so they could sell the acres of prime real estate and make a profit.

Did Rev. Mien E. Miser feel overwhelmed by the large size of his new church and feel compelled to reduce it? Comments from a number of former congregants supported this theory.

A big unanswered question is this: where did the former congregants go? Did they go to another church of the same denomination, go to a different denomination, or did they quit active participation in any church?

The selection process failed for this church. Forty-plus years of building a congregation and serving the community, wiped out as the result of a failed selection process.

Rick Warren addressed the parking problem in his book *The Purpose-Driven Church*.

> I once asked several pastors of the largest churches in California what their biggest mistake was in building. Every one of them had the same answer: Not enough parking. When people come to church, they like to bring their cars! If you don't have a place for their car, you don't have a place for them. No matter how big your building is, you won't be able to fill it if there isn't enough parking. (1995, page 254)

Where were the church elders, the diocese, and bishop while this self-destruction process was underway? They were charged with representing the needs of the congregation. One viable explanation is that the elders were overcome by the new senior clergy's God complex. He had a strong and forceful persona—and in his case, a big misused ego! However, he had attended seminary and been anointed by the bishop. He was ordained. He must know what he is doing. He may have been a theological genius, but he was not proficient at church management and public relations.

Lessons Learned: The church elders failed to rein him in! The elders, bishop, and congregation must stand up to such clergy. It is their church, not the clergy's church. You hire a lawn service to take care of your lawn. It is important to note that the lawn service doesn't own the lawn. If they mow your garden or flower beds and leave piles of grass in your driveway, you may tell them to shape up. Most likely, however, is that you'll tell them to not come back. That same business decision is necessary for unsuitable clergy.

Why did Rev. Mien E. Miser not have his staff get together to discuss the proposed changes? If he had, most of the changes would not have occurred. However, since the staff had been just about eliminated, there was no staff available to discuss the changes. It is important to note that the assistant clergy asked to be reassigned shortly after Rev. Mien E. Miser's arrival because of disagreement with the reverend's actions and management philosophy.

SPRING BUTTS

A full range of opinions created independently, then presented to the full group, often results in a superior solution. Society is made up of many types of personalities. They range from extreme extroverts to extreme introverts—and all play a vital role in civilization. This free-thinking method helps prevent a groupthink solution that is influenced by those that one lady calls "spring butts." Other terms for *spring butts* include *face timers* and *high blirters*. Dylan Evans's book *Risk Intelligence* references a study at the University of Texas that clearly describes this type of student.

> In one study, they found that classmates of high blirters were impressed with them early in the semester, but that their favorable opinions waned as the course progressed ... because blirtatiousness is not associated with intelligence, their classmates came to realize that the exuberance of some high blirters can exceed their insightfulness. (2012, page 108)

Lessons Learned: Just because someone feels compelled to always give their opinion first doesn't mean it's a good one. Some spring butts are so confident and wedded to their opinions that they will try to stifle other opinions. Remember the Bay of Pigs and the LBJ vignettes. It's important to hear all opinions.

CLERGY LADY

The music program was running well in the church. The music director had a nice choir, and music was rehearsed one to two months in advance. Rehearsing a piece for four to six weeks helped compensate for members missing a rehearsal. By the time the piece was used in the service, the members should have been able to rehearse it multiple times.

Enter a new senior clergy, who was also a vocalist. Clergy Lady really liked to sing in the choir—but without coming to rehearsals. She was too busy to attend rehearsals, even the Sunday preservice rehearsal; the role of senior clergy was rather demanding. However, she would regularly join the choir during the service. Unfortunately, her last-minute unrehearsed membership in the choir usually proved detrimental to the quality of the choir's performance.

Well, Clergy Lady had a solution for that. After several months of being a Last-Minute-Jane, she gave a large stack of music to the director and said, "This is the music we'll do for the rest of the year."

It was music that Clergy Lady knew. That way, the choir would be able to adjust more efficiently to her musical dictates. After several months of Clergy Lady running the choir, as well as being clergy, the music director finally came to the conclusion that he was not compatible with Clergy Lady. It was time to say goodbye and seek another position, which he did, in December, after giving a two-month notice.

The following May, Clergy Lady was removed from the church. Her performance had finally reached the point of being unacceptable to the selectors (diocese or church elders).

Lessons Learned: Clergy Lady apparently wanted to be a music leader. If she liked the choir that much, she should have gone the music career route. She chose the wrong career path. The selection process also failed. Depending on the denomination, the selection failure rested with the diocese, the local search committee, or the church elders.

After she was hired, and several episodes of last-minute choir membership, the church elders should have had a polite chat with Clergy Lady. Clergy Lady should have been told you lead the congregation in worship and the music leader leads the congregation in singing and provides service music. Join the choir a few times a year, but let the musicians do their job.

Apparently, Clergy Lady didn't receive that message until after the music director had resigned. The result was everyone lost. The church lost a good music director and presumably a good clergy. Both the music director and Clergy Lady had to find new employment. It was a lose-lose-lose situation. No one was a winner.

One possible option for Clergy Lady, if she had such strong feelings to fill the roles of clergy and music, would be to start her own church from scratch. In her start-from-scratch church, she could have served both roles at the same time. The congregants would know what to expect. The result would have been a win-win for everyone.

Another option would be for Clergy Lady to start a new service in the church where she would be the musician as well as the clergy. Perhaps a relaxed contemporary service.

It is important to note that there are numerous clergy with musical talent. I know one who plays in a community band. A few play their guitar at a contemporary guitar service several times a month. With some searching and creative thinking, there are numerous musical opportunities for such clergy.

SUMMARY

The best decisions are predominantly group decisions, or decisions in which all the pros and cons have been presented and evaluated. One of the customs in the military is that the lowest-ranking individuals voice their ideas and opinions first.

A friend did this with his reserve military unit, and an NCO with an oversized ego complained to him about it. Sergeant Big Ego said the officer should have asked for his opinion first so the lower ranks would know what to say.

Don't let someone with a big ego stifle the presentation of all information—both for and against an issue, item, or proposal. Rev. Al Waze Wright did this to the detriment of the church. Clergy Lady made a unilateral decision to sing in the choir each

Sunday but never make a rehearsal. Her oversized music ego caused the music director to leave and led to her dismissal from the church. A big misused ego hurts; it does not help.

Presenting the pros and cons, and specifically encouraging members with dissenting opinions to be heard, will usually prove quite beneficial. First, the minority opinions will be heard, and quite possibly result in modifying the final decision. Second, the culture will evolve that encourages full discussion prior to a decision being made. Bad decisions will still be made, but the number will be significantly reduced.

As stated earlier, when opinions are being requested in a meeting, it is wise to start with the junior staff members and progress upward to the leader. The purpose is to avoid stifling the thoughts of the junior members.

— 3 —

ARROGANCE

I'm starting this chapter with a few nonchurch vignettes to give examples of *arrogance*. The church vignettes will follow.

GENERAL MANAGER

There was a large, well-to-do community with community owned and managed facilities. These facilities included golf, tennis, gym, swimming, dining, and a sports bar.

The food and beverage segment over the years had built up a nice financial cushion. This cushion was intended to provide continuity during hard times due to hurricanes, blizzards, COVID, etc. The agreement was that food and beverage prices would be reduced if the financial cushion became too large.

The general manager, however, had a better idea. He decided that he would just reallocate the food and beverage cushion funds to another area that "needed" additional funds. The manager of the "needing" area had a weakness; it was budget management. The result was the "needing" area was always short of funds. That manager spent what he didn't have, then asked for more after the fact. I'm sure you, the reader, know people who live paycheck to paycheck, eat out regularly, have a recent-model car, and always wear very nice clothes. However, they quickly spend their tax refund and then complain about high prices and their need for a better-paying job.

As to be expected, some members complained, and the general manager's response was phrased quite elegantly and saturated with diplo-speak; it would have made a career politician envious. It went something like this: "I've looked at the big picture and what is best for the entire organization. I've talked with other general managers of similar organizations. I even discussed the issue with a well-known consultant friend who did *not* charge for her opinion. I even evaluated the cost of tea in China against our beverage prices and found our prices are quite suitable. And although the phrase is often overused, you have to break some eggs to make an omelet. Unfortunately, we had to break some eggs for the benefit of everyone.

What he said is essence was "I'm the general manager. I'm smarter that you. I always know best."

Golly! That sounds very similar to the responses some of our elected officials in Washington, DC, give when asked a pointed question.

Lessons Learned: I expect the community had a council, or some board of representatives, that could, or should, have expressed a concern. Bureaucrats have a tendency to push the limits of their power, often assuming power that they don't have. This is what happened here. Money was moved from one area to another area against the rules/charter of the community. It was a rob-Peter-to-pay-Paul solution. Since it, apparently, was known that the manager of the needing area had weak budget management skills, why wasn't he replaced? Or why wasn't he given budget management guidance by the general manager?

Unfortunately, the result was that the incompetent manager would continue making poor budget management decisions, the general manager would continue robbing Peter to pay Paul, and the members would continue to complain. However, the precedent had been set; robbing Peter to pay Paul was kinda acceptable, or rather acceptable.

COURT MARTIAL

Way back in the twentieth century, when I was in the air force, I sat on the board of a general court martial. There were seven officers on the board: lieutenants, captains, majors, and one lieutenant colonel. The prosecution and defense presented their cases. The board was given their instructions and then went into closed session. The board of a court martial is the equivalent of a jury; they decide the fate of the accused.

A secret vote was taken, and the findings were five to convict and two not to convict. At this point, the next step would be to discuss the merits for not guilty and merits for guilty. Before this step was taken, however, the lieutenant colonel stood up and forcefully expressed his opinion for conviction. Then he proceeded to threaten the careers of anyone foolish enough to express their opinion to not convict. He was a bully. He used his rank to intimidate the opinions of the lower ranks. "Vote my way or I'll make you wish you had! I'm right. Look at the silver leaves on my shoulder." He was arrogant.

Note: The seven members of the board are all equal; rank has no bearing in the decision. A lieutenant's vote is equal to a colonel's vote. The lieutenant colonel should have presented his case somewhat like this: "I'm older and have quite a bit of life wisdom. I feel the accused should be found guilty because—" And then he should proceed to explain his reasoning. The dissenting board members would then proceed to explain why they thought the accused should be found not guilty.

Lessons Learned: Several members of the board, independently, went to the legal office and reported the bully's intimidating rant. The colonel displayed *arrogance*. Most people probably experience moments of *arrogance* during their lives. Most, however, realize what is happening, or someone tells them that they're being *arrogant*, and they change their behavior. People are imperfect; they make mistakes. After all, they are human.

In this case, for whatever reason, the colonel didn't, or couldn't, understand what he was doing. He was transferred shortly thereafter. Good guys 1: bully 0.

PERFORMANCE REPORT

Nassim Taleb's book *Black Swan: The Impact of the Highly Improbable,* has an anecdote about a trader for a large investment bank. The trader, Nero, had a meeting with his supervisor for the annual evaluation.

> Nero found the evaluation absurd because it did not so much judge the quality of a trader's performance as encourage him to game the system by working for short-term profits at the expense of possible blowups ... So, one day early in his career, Nero sat down and listened very calmly to the evaluation of his "supervisor." When Nero was handed the evaluation form, he tore it into small pieces in front of him. He did this very slowly, accentuating the contrast between the nature of the act and the tranquility with which he tore the

paper. The boss watched him blank with fear, eyes popping out of his head. Nero focused on his undramatic, slow-motion act, elated by both the feeling of standing up for his beliefs and the aesthetics of its execution. The combination of elegance and dignity was exhilarating. He knew that he would either be fired or left alone. He was left alone. (2007, page 99)

What is the purpose of a performance report? To check a box, to keep the employee in line, to make the supervisor feel in charge, or to assure the employee is doing everything to help and improve the organization?

Keep the above anecdote in mind as you read the following, related to me by a former staff member of a medium-sized church of a major denomination.

DENOMINATIONAL TENETS

Rev. Hoity Toity, with years of experience at other churches, had been the senior clergy at his new church for only a few months. At a staff meeting, he said he was not going to follow one of the tenets of the denomination. He proceeded to issue a new policy that was in direct conflict with the church's tenets.

The result was that his assistant clergy was horrified at his openly flouting one of the denomination's tenets. She went to the diocese and arranged for an immediate transfer to another church in the state. The denomination was short of clergy, and Rev. Hoity Toity had many years of service and gave outstanding sermons. And I also I expect he had a comfortable retirement account accrued. While one can only surmise as to what the reverend was thinking, I'm sure his thoughts were the same as Nero, the trader.

I'll either be cashiered by the church, or they'll leave me alone. I believe they'll leave me alone. The church left him alone.

While Nero was concerned about avoiding a negative impact on his employer, the investment bank, Rev. Hoity Toity wasn't. His actions resulted in a marked drop in church attendance. But apparently, he didn't care; he had his retirement package.

Lessons Learned: The selection process failed. The diocesan selection or the search committee didn't successfully vet Rev. Toity. Once ensconced in the church, the elders, diocese, or the congregation should have had a tenets-of-the-denomination chat with Rev. Hoity Toity. I believe the elders and congregation automatically assumed that he was an ordained clergy and thus knew how to run a church. Perhaps church doctrine should have been a requirement in the vetting process.

TAKE THIS JOB AND SHOVE IT

The senior clergy really didn't like the music director at all. There's nothing wrong with that; personality conflicts are a part of life. Most folks, however, recognize this and establish a peaceful coexistence. Both parties usually follow the "You be nice to me and I'll be nice to you" philosophy. This particular senior clergy, however, didn't embrace that philosophy.

As the year progressed, the senior clergy became more outspoken during the service about what he perceived were shortcomings of the music director. Finally, the music director had had enough and in the middle of a service turned to the senior clergy and said, "I've had enough of your garbage. Take this job and shove it," and then walked out, in front of a shocked congregation.

The music director went to another city and got another job, at a higher salary. The response of the congregation varied. A significant number left and attended another house of worship, a suitable majority remained, a few stopped participating in any religious service, and a small number now attend another church only on special occasions.

Lessons Learned: Relationships among church leadership and church staff need to be respectful.

SCHOOL NAME CHANGE

This vignette is not about a church. However, it is an excellent example of some individuals getting all puffed up with self-importance based on their title. It is a great example of *arrogance*.

The school board concluded that the name of the school should be changed. The current name was not to their liking. The change was discussed and citizens of the school district were asked for suggestions. There were meetings, discussions on radio talk shows, local articles in the newspaper, etc. Suggestions were sent in and three names ranked quite high. Those names were printed on a ballot and the voters in the school district voted. The votes were counted and one name was the obvious winner.

Democracy at work? Well, maybe, maybe not. The citizens have spoken. The school board, however, knew that the voters were not able to really understand the issue. The school board then selected a new name that wasn't even on the ballot. As one would expect, the voters were stunned. The school board was shocked that the voters weren't pleased with their decision. After all, "We're the school board. We know best!"

Lessons Learned: The school board orchestrated a public relations charade. Why go through the process of gaining input, submitting the proposed names to the voters, only to ignore the outcome? The school board's action is an excellent example of arrogance, oversized egos, and *"Godfather* Management," which is the title of the next chapter.

Note: At the time of this writing, a group of citizens had filed a lawsuit against members of the school board.

STEEPLE CHASE

Once upon a time, in a town someplace in the United States, lived two sisters: Ms. Heighen Meighty and Ms. Behtern Meighty. Incidentally, the sisters had recently inherited a very large amount of money; they were now independently wealthy. In that situation, the vast majority of people would enjoy a good life and do interesting things with the money, such as starting a business, travel, giving to various charities, helping the poor, investing the funds, or improving the lives of other people. In other words, do good deeds.

Unfortunately, a dark cloud came over the town, and some evil crept into the hearts of the two sisters. When the dark cloud left, the two sisters were on the outs with each other. The result was that Ms. Behtern Meighty left the church and joined another church in town. No way was she going to be in the same church as that sister of hers, Ms. Heighen Meighty.

Ms. Heighen Meighty decided to improve the image of the church she attended since her sister was no longer a member. Heighen Meighty's regular contributions to the church were very important to its existence. She talked with the elders and the clergy and strongly urged them to increase the height of the church steeple. Recognizing that the hand that feeds needs to be kept happy, the clergy and elders agreed that a taller steeple was just what the church needed—especially since Ms. Heighen Meighty would pay for it. Construction began immediately to increase the height of the church steeple. Within a month, the church attended by Ms. Heighen Meighty had the tallest steeple in town. And Ms. Heighen Meighty's checkbook was now appreciably thinner.

Ms. Behtern Meighty was deeply hurt. "That terrible sister of mine is thumbing her nose at me with that tall steeple. I have a reputation to uphold. I won't stand for such snootiness. I'll show her."

Ms. Behtern Meighty met with the clergy and elders of her new church and explained the situation, while holding her fat checkbook up so everyone could see it. "Our church steeple is really on the short side. It should be raised. This church needs to be a beacon of light for the town. Why, we might even be able to rent space in the steeple as a cell phone tower. Besides, I'll foot the bill."

And it came to pass that Ms. Behtern Meighty's church now had the tallest steeple in town. One-up-woman-steeple-ship had been won by Ms. Behtern Meighty.

Lessons Learned: Not sure, but money speaks. Both sisters had an issue with ego and arrogance. And in this case, money spoke at two churches.

And you thought this vignette was going to be about horses.

SUMMARY

If arrogance is not challenged, it will spread and become accepted. As each day passes and we slowly increase our speed on a smooth stretch of highway, we start to feel that doing fifty miles per hour in a thirty miles per hour zone is OK. That's what the police are for. If you're lucky, you get a warning; if you're not so lucky, you get a ticket. In some states, exceeding the speed limit by twenty miles per hour is considered a felony. Don't ask me why; ask the state legislatures.

Rev. Hoity Toity's arrogance led him to flout a tenet of his denomination and drive the assistant clergy away. The take-this-job-and-shove-it clergy's arrogance to continually denigrate the music director during the service hurt everyone. The "steeple chase" ladies only hurt themselves, but what a waste of money. They missed an opportunity to do some real good with their inheritance.

The elders, or congregation, should have stepped in early and very diplomatically told the arrogant ones that such behavior is not acceptable. Arrogance can lead to bullying. Such individuals usually back down when their arrogance and bullying are challenged. And it's quite possible that the arrogant ones don't even realize that they're being arrogant.

Godfather management and dictators are a part of the real world, as you'll see in the next chapter.

— 4 —

GODFATHER MANAGEMENT

Godfather management is a step above arrogance. It's important to remember that no one is perfect. Everyone has their character flaws and idiosyncrasies.

In the 1965 comical movie *Those Magnificent Men and Their Flying Machines*, a pre-WWI Prussian officer has been forced to ditch his plane in the English Channel. As he and his airplane are slowly sinking, the officer is reading an instruction book on flying and says out loud to himself something like "I'm a Prussian officer. I can do anything."

This I-can-do-anything syndrome infects almost everyone at some time in their life. Clergy, bishops, and at times, the church elders have been infected.

But first, a brief detour to talk about dictators, then church vignettes. The reverend in the upcoming vignette, "Dump the Music Director," experienced this I-can-do-anything syndrome, and he wasn't a Prussian officer flying an airplane.

DICTATORS

Some individuals have the charisma to get the majority of individuals to agree with their way of thinking. Adolf Hitler used his charisma and lies, reinforced by his brownshirt thugs, as well as assassinations, to help become the leader of Germany. He knew he was right; many of those who disagreed with him learned that wasn't a good thing to do.

Napoleon knew he was destined to be the leader of France, and the rest of Europe. He was the smartest soldier and general at the time; just ask him. He could only win. He knew he could not fail. So he invaded Russia. Unfortunately for Napoleon, and fortunately for Europe, Napoleon failed to conquer Russia.

Joseph Stalin emerged from the Russian Revolution of the early 1900s as the leader of the Soviet Union. Those who didn't obey died. (Trotsky was assassinated in Mexico; Lenin died under suspicious circumstances.) Millions of peasants died of starvation when Stalin took their food. He controlled the military, and in the 1930s he purged the military of its best leaders. He discovered that purge idea was a big oopsie when Hitler invaded Russia.

When individuals are elected or appointed (I'm sure a few manage through other means) and arrive at a leadership position, they do their best to perform well and not abuse their newfound authority and power. Some examples of these positions include school board members, congressmen, district attorneys, judges, homeowners' associations, etc. While the vast majority perform admirably in their positions, unfortunately some let it go to their head. These very few individuals suddenly believe that they are smarter than everyone else. The dictator gene suddenly surfaces and they start creating and implementing their own agenda, not the agenda of the people they're supposed to represent. Keep the dictator-gene-run-amuck in mind as you read the following vignettes.

DUMP THE MUSIC DIRECTOR

Rev. Demigh Gawd was new to the church. He quickly concluded that the music director, a longtime member of the church, was not to his liking. Rev. Demigh Gawd was a "neaty," and the music director was a "messy." It was an *Odd Couple* arrangement (from the 1970s TV series), a Felix Unger and Oscar Madison pair. The obvious, and proper, solution would be for Rev. Demigh Gawd to call in the music director in January or February and inform him that at the end of this season (usually May or June), "I'll no longer need your services. Update your résumé and start your search for a new position. In June, I'll provide you with the usual three months' severance pay."

Instead, Rev. Gawd elected to build a case against the director. He felt it was a smart move since the music director was very popular. He implemented his own prejudicial ten-step program of music director removal.

Step 1: The reverend created a choir questionnaire that he brought to a rehearsal. The questionnaire centered around the capability of the director. The choir said he was doing a good job, and they liked him. However, that wasn't the answer Rev. Demigh Gawd desired.

Step 2: A few weeks later, the reverend brought questionnaire number 2 to a choir rehearsal. Again, the response was that the director was doing a good job and they liked him.

Wow, thought the reverend. *The choir just doesn't understand how they're supposed to answer.*

Step 3: The following week, questionnaire number 3 was given to the choir, again with the same results. This time, however, the choir asked Rev. Demigh Gawd why he was harassing the choir director. The reverend (with his hands behind his back and fingers crossed) replied that he was only trying to assure that everyone was satisfied with the music program.

Step 4: The reverend went back to the drawing board; it was time for a new plan. This time the reverend created a music commission. The commission held meetings and asked choir members the biased questions provided by Rev. Demigh Gawd. Following is an example of a biased question:

> Neutral: What do you think about the pink and purple polka dots on the front door of the church?
>
> Biased: Don't you feel that pink and purple polka dots on the front door of the church are rather outlandish?

Step 5: The commission complained that the music director hadn't come to their meetings. The music director replied that Rev. Gawd had told him *not* to attend the meetings.

Step 6: The commission, trying to get answers, was told to give the questions to the music director, who would then give the answers to Rev. Gawd, which he did. However, the reverend always forgot and never passed the answers on to the commission.

At last, things are starting to work my way, concluded Rev. Demigh Gawd.

Step 7: *It worked in that Godfather movie*, thought the reverend. *I'll modify that approach to my church. Well, I can't put a horse's head in the music director's bed; it wouldn't be easy to get into his house. However, it is easy to get into his office.* Even though the door to the music director's office was locked, on many Monday mornings an anonymous note would appear on the director's desk. The anonymous notes would critique the music at Sunday's service as being too long, too loud, too fast, a member of the volunteer choir off pitch, etc.

This is going quite well, thought the reverend, *but I need to build a stronger case.*

Step 8: Since choir members were sometimes absent due to sickness, business travel, school events, bad weather, etc., some Sunday mornings the choir could unexpectedly be rather thin. In anticipation of such an occurrence, the director always had an easy backup offertory anthem ready, if needed, to use at the last minute. Many music directors do this; it serves as a musical life preserver in the event of a miniscule Sunday choir turnout.

So many weeks later, the reverend showed the music director a letter, with the congregant's name removed, complaining that the offertory was not what was printed in the bulletin. The anonymous letter stated that the entire service was ruined when the music listed in the bulletin was not performed. The sender stated that she was so devastated that she was unable to eat and could not have Sunday brunch with her friends.

Step 9: Concluding that the time was now ripe to dump the music director, Rev. Demigh Gawd sent the director to a two-week summer church music seminar, at church expense.

Step 10: Upon his return in July, however, Rev. Gawd called him in and said, "I have an offer you can't refuse. Give me a letter of resignation stating that you have decided to leave your position as music director, and I'll give you three months' severance pay. You can continue through the end of the month. If you refuse, however, you must leave right now, not go to your office for personal items, and you will *not* receive any severance pay. Which is your choice?"

Note: The ideal time to release unflattering news is at 5:00 p.m. on the Friday before a three-day weekend. Politicians do it all the time. July and August are the ideal months to make unpopular church changes.

Rev. Gawd really had a bad case of the I-don't-like-you-itus. He let his personal animosity toward the music director besmirch the reputation of the church. His goal was to hurt the music director, not just say goodbye to him. A rather sad testament to his failure to understand his religious training and let his personal pettiness control his decisions.

PS: The music director chose the obvious; he provided a letter of resignation and received the severance pay.

The following chart shows the usual months for interviews and hiring of music and choir director positions:

Resign	Résumé updating	Summer	New
Retire	Interview/Hiring	Doldrums	Season
Jan/Feb/Mar	Mar/Apr/May/Jun	Jun/Jul/Aug	Sep

The result, and most likely the intended result, was that the music director was dumped into the unemployed status in August with little chance of employment the coming year. Remember it is easier to find a job while you're still employed.

OH, BY THE WAY

Rev. Demigh Gawd was quite relieved. Just a final meeting with that music director, that messy Oscar Madison of music, and he'd be gone—forever!

Step 11, a bonus: The music director had completed his last service on Sunday. It was Monday, and at the appointed hour, he met with the reverend for the exit interview. Rev. Demigh Gawd said, "The month of August should be an excellent month to find a new position. And by the way, never come back to this church again!"

Note: As presented in the chart earlier, church music positions are usually announced and filled in March, April, May, and June. They are almost all filled by June and July, and at the latest by early August. This was another way in which Rev. Demigh Gawd was able to vent his dislike of the music director. It was also a way to punish him.

Several weeks later, a lady congregant with very deep financial pockets saw the former music director in the supermarket. She asked him if he had really departed voluntarily. When he replied, "No," she stated that she was not going to give another penny to the church.

Remember nothing stays secret forever. When someone is treated unfairly, the truth will eventually come out. As a sergeant once told me, "The only way to keep a secret is for only one person to know it."

A new choir director was hired, and she was highly qualified. She did great things for the music program. Unfortunately, Rev. Demigh Gawd started the same *Godfather* management methods with her. He left notes on her desk Monday mornings, blanked out letters from anonymous church members, etc. She departed in two years and moved to another town and church where her exceptional talents were appreciated.

Lessons Learned: This was an arrogant *Godfather* model clergy in action. It's rather unlikely that none of the church elders knew what Rev. Demigh Gawd was doing. The elders should have intervened. If, by a stroke of luck, Rev. Demigh Gawd kept his intentions and plan secret, the elders and/or the diocese should have intervened after the fact and made amends to the music director and appropriately admonished the reverend. If the elders did so, they didn't tell me, and they shouldn't tell me either.

I DON'T ANSWER TO THE CITY!

Rev. Buv De Lauh wanted more parking spaces in the church parking lot. On Sundays, the congregants parked in an adjacent business park and entered through the back of the church building, walking past the Sunday school classrooms.

The reverend expressed the parking issue to the congregation. And like most congregations, there was a large assortment of professions and businesses represented.

A congregant who was an experienced commercial developer researched the situation and provided the reverend with his findings. While the suggested changes appeared logical, they would violate the city code.

The reverend thanked the developer for the information and thought about it, but he didn't think about it too long.

Rev. Buv De Lauh contacted a parking lot striping company to have new stripes painted. When the company asked if the changes met city code, Rev. Buv De Lauh replied, "Go ahead and make the changes. I've already had that researched."

Lessons Learned: As a religious leader, he should be held to a higher standard. In this case, for apparently self-importance, he decided to flout the zoning requirements.

A general once explained to me that regulations are for his guidance. If he decides to do something contrary to regulations, he'd better have a very good reason. Did Rev. Buv De Lauh have a very good reason? Did he take the position that begging forgiveness was more practical than asking permission? The more probable explanation is that he was practicing *Godfather* management.

MAKE IT YOUR IDEA TO LEAVE

Rev. I. M. Gawd was new to the church and was rather puffed up with his title of senior clergy and the perceived authority that came with it. He had an immediate dislike for the assistant clergy who had been at the church for several years.

On his second day on the job, as is the tradition in that denomination, the assistant clergy came to him with a letter of resignation effective in ninety days. The letter stated the obvious, that it was tradition for the assistant clergy to resign. That would permit the new senior clergy to select an assistant that he would be most comfortable to work with.

Friday afternoon of that same week (the first week), Rev. I. M. Gawd called her in and said she was to resign within the month, and he would give her one month's severance pay. Further, her letter of resignation was to state that it was her idea to leave. If she failed to do so, she was to leave within the hour and there would be no severance pay. "And yes, I know you're a widow with a child to support."

Wow! Rev. I. M. Gawd really felt a need to flex his new muscles. He wanted his way, right now! One congregant suggested he probably gave very good temper tantrums as a child and usually got his way. *Godfather* management in action.

Lessons Learned: The elders and the diocese should have intervened and had a true come-to-Jesus meeting with the new clergy. In hindsight, one can see how successful an arrogant *Godfather* management decision can be when the elders and the diocese fail to intervene.

Rick Warren explains the necessity of standing up for what is just and proper very well in *The Purpose-Driven Life*.

> Peacemaking is also not *appeasement*. Always giving in, acting like a doormat, and allowing others to always run over you is not what Jesus had in mind. He refused to back down on many issues, standing his ground in the face of evil opposition. (2002, page 153)

It is important to note that one of the elders did stand up for the assistant clergy and got the assistant clergy three months' severance pay. Unfortunately, Rev. I. M. Gawd was really a mismatch for this church, and perhaps he was in the wrong profession.

Rev. I. M. Gawd planned ahead when he signed on as senior clergy; he finagled a five-year contract. He had his employment set.

The church let him go at the end of his contract. The unjust treatment of the assistant clergy was just one of several actions that led to his departure.

With hindsight, perhaps the elders should have had a "You've failed to properly fulfill you contract" talk with him. "We don't like what you've done. Shape up or you're fired—contract or no contract!"

PS: the church elders vowed to never again issue such a long contract.

LARGE MEMORIAL SERVICE

A widow was planning the memorial service and reception for her late husband who was well-known and had held some high positions during his life. She was well experienced in the area of estimating attendance at receptions and conferences. She estimated that about 350 to four hundred family and friends would attend the memorial service. The sanctuary of her church had a capacity of only a little over two hundred.

She talked with Rev. Ima Climber about doing the memorial service at a larger church of the same denomination. The reverend made some calls and said such a church had been found. The widow was preparing to send out the announcement with time and location, so she called the reverend to reconfirm the information. This is a variation of the carpenter's measure twice-and-cut-once rule.

Rev. Climber called back a few minutes later and said the other church had a conflict but the service could be held at Rev. Climber's church. "Besides, you're under stress and you have really overestimated the attendance. Actual attendance will only be around one hundred."

The widow explained that her estimate of 350 to four hundred was realistic. Additionally, the posted fire code notice set the limit at 210. Rev. Climber replied, "Well, we just won't tell the fire marshal."

The widow knew better. A clergy friend at another church made a reservation for her at a larger church of the same denomination. Attendance for the memorial service was over four hundred.

Later it came out that Rev. Ima Climber was in the résumé-building process. The widow theorized that the reverend wanted to be able to include such a large memorial service on her list of unique accomplishments. Within a year, Rev. Climber had climbed up to bishop in another state.

Lessons Learned: The clergy needs to listen to the congregant. The congregant may be wrong; the congregant may be right. If Rev. Climber had asked how the widow arrived at her figures, she would have understood that 350 to four hundred was a realistic estimate. Remember in this situation, the wishes of the widow should come first, even if actual attendance turns out to be about one hundred.

A natural tendency is to reach a conclusion before hearing the facts. In this case, Rev. Climber, based on her experience, quickly reached a conclusion about the number of attendees without hearing the widow's explanation. It's important to delay reaching a decision. Rev. Climber should have been skeptical of her attendance numbers and the widow's numbers. Always consider other possibilities. Gather all the facts. Verify the facts.

It is important to remember it is the widow's event, not the clergy's event. However, clergy are tasked to guide, especially someone who is emotionally vulnerable. Thus, the clergy can really be perched on the horns of a dilemma.

YANKEE, GO HOME

The seminarian was well into his seminary training. A part of his training was assisting in worship services. Every month, he went before a progress committee that asked him questions regarding his progress. At these monthly meetings, the seminarian was told that he was doing a good job, he was on right track, and to keep up the good work.

This continued for many months. At the end of the assessment period, the seminarian would go for his last meeting with a new committee—the final committee.

The forthcoming meeting was the culmination of the monthly meetings. The committee would give their recommendation regarding his ordination. After all, the soon-to-be clergy had checked all the boxes and passed the reviews of the progress committee.

Well, almost all the boxes. There was one final box that

the final committee kept secret. And it was a box the progress committee was not permitted to see.

On the day the seminarian was to have the meeting with the final committee, the candidate arrived at the appointed time. A member of the final committee came out and said, "You are not one of the cousins here. You're a Yankee. You're not welcome here. Go home!"

Lessons Learned: The good-old-boy network really had a mean streak. Why didn't they tell the Yankee seminarian that he wasn't a fit for their diocese and that he should go to another diocese for his one-year assessment?

Why did the diocese permit him to enroll if they had no intention of following through with ordination? Or maybe the diocese was not aware that this particular committee didn't like Yankees. The Civil War, the War between the States, the War of Northern Aggression, the Great Unpleasantness continues.

Or was the "Yankee, go home" message the decision of the committee or just one arrogant member of the committee? I lean heavily toward it being the decision of just one member of the committee.

Hmmmmmm. Certainly not very Christian-like, was it?

All professions have some bad apples. Just as there are bad cops, bad lawyers, bad doctors, and bad teachers, there are also bad members of evaluation committees.

NO NEW HIRES

It was a medium-sized church with two assistant clergy, a music director, and an assistant music director. As occurs in all organizations, members will retire or leave the organization. The assistant music director resigned and headed off to a greener pasture.

Rev. Fork Ed Tung told the music director, "Write a new job description for your assistant and we'll refill the position." The music director did so and was told that if he knew of potential candidates, ask them to apply.

Several qualified candidates contacted the church to apply and were told that there were no openings at that time. The music director inquired at the church office and was told that all new hires were temporarily on hold. No explanation as why was provided.

During this period, the music director was responsible for eleven separate music groups. Additional inquiries about the replacement were met with vague explanations but that the position would be advertised shortly.

Rev. Fork Ed Tung stalled for nine months, so the position was never filled. During that time, the music director was criticized for not having an assistant. Members of his music groups (and musicians from other churches) pitched in to assist him while waiting for the never-to-arrive assistant. With perseverance and help from members of his music groups, the music director managed to significantly increase the size of the choir, almost doubled the size of a semiannual festival choir the church sponsored, and doubled the size and quality of the church's once-a-month orchestra. Shortly thereafter, the music director was quietly, rudely, and unceremoniously terminated in the middle of the summer. The terminated music director was quickly replaced with a full-time music director and several well-qualified part-time assistants.

It later came out that Rev. Fork Ed Tung never intended to hire an assistant music director. The whole no-new-hires policy was a ruse. The real purpose was to make the music director so miserable carrying the workload of two people that he would give up in frustration and leave voluntarily. Unfortunately, the character of the music director rose to meet the challenge as well as maintain and improve the music program at the church. The music director saw his position as a calling, not a job.

Lessons Learned: This is a tough one, many possible lessons here. The one question that stands out to me is this: why didn't the elders intervene early on? Were the elders aware that Rev. Fork Ed Tung had issues that should be addressed? If they were observant and aware of what was happening in the church, they certainly should have been aware of Rev. Fork Ed Tung's weird policies. I'm confident that you, the reader, can probably come up with other preventive solutions.

SUMMARY

All puffed up with their self-importance, their defiant pompousness, and their chosen path to deliberately hurt others through their I-know-I'm-right attitude, their I'm-all-powerful and *Godfather* management method becomes a one-lane highway to their malevolent goal.

Reverent Demigh Gawd in Dump the Music Director, spent a lot of time and brain power creating a "case." In my opinion, he enjoyed the process of building a case to justify firing the music director. As stated in "Lessons Learned," it would have much easier to just tell the music director in January to find a new job.

Rev. Buv De Lauh deliberately flouted city code, because he wanted to. With the additional Sunday parking in the adjacent business park, he had no need to restripe the church parking lot in violation of city code.

Rev. I. M. Gawd overrode church policy and bullied the assistant into resigning early, and by the way, Make It Your Idea to Leave. He didn't want to wait three months; he wanted his way *now!* He probably gave very good temper tantrums as a child to get his way. The assistant clergy must be commended for not inflicting pain on the body of Rev. Gawd. If she had, and there was a trial, and I was on the jury, I would vote her actions justifiable.

A church has a lot of moving parts. Congregants give their time to make things work. Some staff members are hired to fill some positions. With qualified people in all the positions and led by an ordained clergy, how could church management go wrong? You'll find out in the next chapter.

— 5 —
CHURCH MANAGEMENT

A few background nonchurch vignettes before the church vignettes.

ENTREPRENEURSHIP

Some individuals have a strong innovative gene. They want to try something another way to do something, what they perceive is a new, improved, and better way. When they fail, their response is often: "Well, I learned another way that doesn't work." Thomas Edison and the light bulb is one example.

Orville Redenbacher spent many years to come up with the best corn for popping.

Michael Dell founded PC Limited, which became Dell Computers.

Innovators and entrepreneurs are vital members of society. This applies to churches, too.

Lessons Learned: Most successful churches add to their services and ministries. They grow, they rarely replace. As you read the vignettes in this book, you'll read about innovative ideas implemented by some churches. Conversely, you'll read about some churches that discontinued or replaced successful services or ministries—to their detriment.

CONTROL

It's important to note that the words management, supervision, and leadership, although different, are often used interchangeably. The words actually have different meanings. However, the successful manager and supervisor are often leaders. A supervisor oversees and directs.

A manager controls expenditures and affairs of an organization, such as a business owner.

A leader motivates people work hard and do the right thing without praise or threat. A leader will work beside an individual to train them to do a specific task. A leader motivates individuals to excel in what they're doing.

Everyone's management style is different. The successful manager has the ability to *control* those under them. Tried and true methods include praise, pats on the back, awards, recognition at staff meetings, and by trusting the employees. Sometimes the trust is misplaced, and a one-on-one chat with the employee resolves the issue. On occasion the individual is just a mismatch for the position, and he, or she, departs for greener pastures. Sometimes, the individual is fired.

A very small percentage of managers *control* the work of their underlings by fear, intimidation, bullying, threats, and negative comments at staff meetings. These supervisors don't trust their employees, and they let the employees know they are not trusted. The great COVID experience that began in 2020 brought about a transformational shift to tele-work, tele-meetings, tele-church, tele-education, tele-medicine, etc. Suddenly, those supervisors that didn't trust their underlings, were forced into the position of increasing the trust of their underlings. Some supervisors failed.

A few managers have the need to physically look at their employees. If they can't line them up and count them, they don't feel in control. Who knows what employees will do if the manager isn't looking at them the entire workday. The vast majority of employees perform their job well without direct oversight. If a problem arises, they seek help from the supervisor; if the supervisor is absent, they'll get guidance from their coworkers. And yes, a few will play hooky and goof-off, thus hurting the organization.

A supervisor directs employees what do to next and often manages his employees.

A leader may manage the organization, and supervise the employees, but a leader also motivates his employees to excel at what they do without supervision. The employees want to excel because that is the right thing to do.

Lessons Learned: Hovercraft management rarely works. Micromanagement rarely works. As you read the vignettes, always think about management style.

Church management is a *team* effort. Remember the cliché, there is no *I* in team.

Almost all successful businesses, organizations, and enterprises have a management structure. Such enterprises include movie stars, rock stars, athletes, and well-known authors. This even includes small partnerships; there is a division of duties.

Whether a partnership or a company, they all have a support staff. A large corporation has vice presidents of finance, marketing, manufacturing, research, public relations, etc. Many large corporations also have a board of directors.

The well-established church has individuals in charge of various functions, such as building maintenance, finance, education, music, fellowship, etc. The church elders can be compared to a board of directors, a city council, or the US Congress.

The congregation of most churches will usually have individuals whose skills include finance, landscaping, music, construction, medical, etc. These individuals have real world experience in their profession and are a valuable source of skills needed for successful church management. It is important, however, that the senior clergy, staff, and the church elders work together when making decisions affecting the church. Keep this in mind (especially finance) as you read the following vignettes.

MONEY TO BE SPENT

The church had a mature congregation and was financially comfortable. The building was in good condition, and there were substantial cash reserves. The previous reverend had retired, and the new reverend arrived.

Rev. Spenn D. Thriff knew he was destined to help churches improve their image. His résumé listed the great things he had done at his previous churches. Each new church was impressed by the image projects he had implemented. Rev. Spenn D. Thriff was climbing the ladder of success. He was really moving up in the world to bigger and bigger churches.

Incidentally, the churches he helped with their image

initially had comfortable financial capability before he arrived to implement his image improvement projects. However, after he departed, money was usually in short supply.

Rev. Spenn D. Thriff, like everyone, had character traits, and one of his was his self-image. He dressed very nicely, went to fine restaurants, and drove a late model luxury car.

Rev. Spenn D. Thriff quickly saw things to "improve" at his new church. In a short period of time, he used the cash reserves for image improvement projects and activities. His image projects were quite visible to the congregation and the community. He was quite pleased with himself. He had completed his mission; it was time for him to move on. There were other churches that needed his skill and knowledge to start image improvement projects.

After he left, the financial drain of the image projects was realized by the church elders. The congregation had to sell their church building and move to a smaller facility. The image improvement projects had almost bankrupted the church. Although a little late in doing so, the elders checked and found out this had occurred at most of his earlier churches, too.

The church elders' role should be similar to a board of directors, and the original role of congress, which is to debate and approve, or disapprove, financial and policy decisions. The elders failed to provide the necessary control over the church finances. The elders had fallen into the fatal misconception that after all, the reverend had been to seminary, so he must know how to run a church.

Had Rev. Spenn D. Thriff slept through financial management classes at seminary? Were there no congregants with business experience? Or were the church elders overcome with the charisma of Rev. Spenn D. Thriff? Were they awed by his anointment by the bishop? He may have been anointed by the bishop, but that anointment did not include blessing him as a financial expert. Well, Rev. Spenn D. Thriff knew how to conduct a worship service, and he also knew how to financially ruin a church

Lessons Learned: Remember if it sounds too good to be true, it probably isn't. The church elders were snookered, they had failed to protect the church. In hindsight, they should have done their homework and thoroughly checked his previous churches before hiring him.

FINANCIAL WISDOM

> Men are born to succeed, not fail. (Henry David Thoreau)

Rev. Dudleigh Dew Wright arrived at his new church. He watched and listened to the church elders and his staff. After a few months, he concluded that the size of the church didn't justify an assistant clergy. The budget was efficient but quite tight. There was little cushion, no rainy-day fund, and any unexpected expense, such as a blizzard, would really hurt the church financially.

Rev. Wright concluded that the assistant clergy position should be eliminated. He discussed his recommendation with the church elders and his assistant clergy. There was a consensus, including agreement by the assistant clergy. The assistant was given a year to find a new position. Fortunately, the assistant quickly found a new position, there was a farewell dinner, and he departed three months later. Once again, it's important to remember that it's always easier to find a new job while you're employed. Compare Rev. Dudleigh Dew Wright with the actions of Rev. Demigh Gawd in "Dump the Music Director."

This termination was done right, and there were no ill

feelings. The church began accumulating some cash reserves and continued to grow and flourish. Eventually, they hired an assistant clergy, but by then, they had sufficient funds to properly support an assistant.

Lessons Learned: The clergy and church staff worked together as they should. The end result was that everyone was a winner.

DIOCESAN RULES

The church had a senior clergy and an assistant clergy. The senior clergy had been there a number of years and applied for a position in another state. The senior clergy interviewed and accepted the new position. Thus, the natural movement of clergy occurred.

Now the church was faced with the need to find a new senior clergy. A search committee was formed. They assembled the list of skills, traits, and other factors that they desired in the perfect senior clergy. Then they accidently committed a no-no. They looked at the assistant clergy who was well liked by the congregation.

Wow! The assistant clergy possessed everything they were looking for in a senior clergy. "Besides, our denomination has a shortage of clergy. We might search for years to find a suitable replacement. Eventually, circumstances might compel us to accept an adequate or a that'll-do candidate as senior clergy. Problem solved." Well, maybe not. The diocese was quite distressed when the elders told them that they had found the perfect candidate—the assistant clergy.

The diocese responded that the church had committed a no-no. Not just a teeny-weeny no-no but a rather big no-no. The tradition was that assistant clergy did *not* move up to the senior clergy position. A new clergy from outside that particular church was to be selected to fill that position. The presumed theory was that new blood and new ideas result in an improved church.

In the army, new commanders almost always come from another unit. Battlefield promotions to commander within the unit only occur when the bureaucracy is dodging bombs and bullets from the enemy.

The church may be directly battling the everyday forces

of evil, but those at the diocesan level believed they needed to manage the larger overall war against evil.

The elders replied that the assistant was everything they wanted, and needed, in a senior clergy. Why go through the search process when the perfect candidate was already at the church? The solution was obvious to the search committee; just promote the assistant clergy to senior clergy.

The bishop replied, "That's not the way it's done in this diocese. We have rules and traditions to follow. Have your search committee go through the process of asking for résumés, calling applicants, interviewing applicants, and in a year or so you will find a suitable senior clergy."

Fortunately for the church, or unfortunately for the diocese, the church had a number of members who were well experienced in working in, with, and around bureaucracies. Those members found the necessary loophole in the diocesan labyrinth of rules and traditions. There was nothing in writing prohibiting elevating the assistant clergy to senior clergy.

"What?" cried the bishop. "That can't be. The diocesan gnomes must have made a mistake. My ego is at stake here; my power must not be challenged."

Sorry, diocese. Your gnomes are the ones that committed the big oopsie. They should have put the no promotion rule in writing.

So that particular church won the battle and the assistant clergy became the new senior clergy. An intelligent decision was upheld and reigned supreme. Good guys = 1: bureaucracy = 0.

Lessons Learned: In this case, it was the diocese that learned the lesson. The gnomes upgraded the written rules to prevent such an intelligent and logical transgression in the future.

The bigger question, however, is this: should the diocese

tradition and rule against promotion from within be retained? Should the diocese allow promotion from within? The assistant clergy certainly knows the congregation and the battles that particular church is waging against the forces of evil.

Fifty years ago, there were more clergy than positions. The no-promotion policy certainly made sense at that time. In the twenty-first century, however, there are more positions than there are clergy.

The diocese position that new blood with fresh eyes and new ideas, not hindered by the we've-always-done-it-this-way blinders, is better for the growth of the church certainly has merit.

In the twenty-first century, however, the real answer is it all depends.

50,000-FOOT VIEW

Using a big picture, what some term a 50,000-foot view, I believe provides an excellent viewpoint of an organization's finances. Irving Janis, in his book *Crucial Decisions*, provides some excellent summations. The follow excerpt describes the ego issue.

> "What's in it for me?" ... "Push for an option that will help me get what I want for myself or for my family." What will happen to the organization is considered to be of secondary importance, if not wholly ignored... (1989, page 66)

A little later, he quotes California State Senator Paul Carpenter in what could be called the empty suit syndrome.

> No person's liberty, property or occupation is safe while the legislature is in session. (1989, page 68)

The decision-making process can determine the increase, or decrease, of good decisions. Remember that the goal is to make good decisions. The objective is to make the best decision possible based on available information, not adequate or that'll-do decisions. Janis provides a hypothesis that I believe is an excellent satellite view of the decision-making process.

> For consequential decisions that implicate vital interests of the organization or nation, deliberate use of a problem-solving approach, with judicious information search and analysis (within the constraints usually imposed by limited organizational resources), will generally result in fewer miscalculations and therefore better outcomes than any other approach. (1989, page 121)

SUMMARY

Management involves the allocating of assets, money, widgets, etc. Some people spend their paycheck as soon as it comes in. They live paycheck to paycheck, buy unnecessary items, and then complain about never having enough money. Others think long term, save for retirement, and establish a rainy-day fund. They create a written budget or have a rather good grasp of where they want their money to go.

Rev. Spenn D. Thriff knew where he wanted the church's money to go, but he didn't think of a budget. He just saw money as something to be spent as he wished, which was on image projects.

Rev. Dew Wright, in stark contrast to Rev. Spenn D. Thriff,

gathered all the facts, discussed the budget with the elders and the assistant clergy, then they made their decision.

Transparency allows the pros and cons to be discussed. A group decision, when all the available facts are known, almost always leads to a better decision. If it is later learned the group decision was a bad decision, there'll be less dissatisfaction because everyone will have had their say.

What are the downstream effects of the decision? Phrased another way, the idea sounds great, but what are the possible, and probable results—the unintended consequences! Rev. Spenn D. Thriff wasn't able to think about the downstream effects. Rev. Dew Wright did and took the necessary action to avoid a crisis in the future.

Consider the following hypothetical church scenario:

1. The seating of the four Sunday services is about 40 percent. It is proposed that the church switch to two services each with about 80 percent seating.
2. Sounds good, but people's lives are now built around the times of the four services.
3. Studies show people feel the pews are full at 70 percent—special services excepted. The result will be a loss of membership.
4. The decision is made to keep the four Sunday services as is.

Remember the famous (or not so famous) axiom "If it ain't broke, don't fix it."

The next chapter starts with a vignette of breaking something so it could be fixed.

— 6 —

CHURCH FINANCIALS

Money is not the root of all evil. People who are bad stewards of other people's money certainly have an evil streak in their personality. Cars don't kill people; drunk drivers kill people. Drunk drivers may be model citizens in most of their life, but that tiny evil streak sneaks in when they've had too much adult beverage when they get in their car.

We give money, time, and talent to our churches. We expect, and have a right to expect, that the money we give is used wisely. Keep that in mind as you read the next two vignettes.

AH, CADILLAC CAR

It was a medium-sized church with about 250 families. The senior clergy retired and the new senior clergy arrived in a Cadillac. The elders asked him why, and Rev. Stu Fud Shertz explained that the car was an investment, not just a car.

The congregation quietly grumbled about the ostentatious car, and a number of members let their opinions be known to the church elders. Well, as one would expect, cars lose their new car smell and new feel after a couple of years. Rev. Stu Fud Shertz required a new Cadillac; after all it was an investment—for the church.

As one would expect, several church members complained to the church elders about the expense. It was explained to them that the elders authorized buying the new car for the clergy. After all, the senior clergy was an important figure in the community that necessitated a car fitting such an exalted position.

The assistant clergy spoke up and expressed his opinion to the senior clergy that such a car wasn't really suitable for a church of their size. Well, that didn't sit well with Rev. Stu Fud Shertz. The assistant was now on the not-so-good side of the reverend.

The new reverend held some opinions—very good opinions since they were his opinions. He strongly advocated for a return of blue laws that would close all stores on Sunday except for grocery stores. The residents, and other churches, firmly rejected his efforts, which lowered his esteem in the community. They explained that many of the citizens worked night shifts and six-day workweeks. For some, Sunday was their only day to shop.

Time marched on and the following year, Rev. Stu Fud Shertz accepted a position in another state.

A sizeable number of the congregation joyfully wished him well, only to find out that the Cadillac went with him. The car was registered in the reverend's name, not in the name of the church. The car was now the reverend's personal automobile.

Lessons Learned: The church elders really failed the church. If Rev. Stu Fud Shertz wanted a Cadillac, that's his choice. But to have the church quietly buy the Cadillac for the reverend, that was the elders' mistake. The elders were snookered. The church was taken to the cleaners. In hindsight, the church was much better off without such an arrogant self-centered clergy. The elders were quite embarrassed and became better stewards of the church's finances in the future.

I'm sure a no-church-car was an item for the vetting of future senior clergy.

PENSION FUND

The little old widow was faithful to her church. She lived next to the church; she had no need for a car. She walked to a nearby grocery store. Her needs were simple, and she was quite frugal. She had a very small pension from her late husband's company. The pay she received from the church was small but adequate for her needs. She was satisfied; she was serving the church.

When the time arrived that she would no longer be able to work full time, she knew things would be OK financially. She had her late husband's social security, his small IRA, and the mortgage on her house would just about be paid off. Add to that the small pension she would receive from her years as the church secretary, and her future was not gloom and doom.

One of the church elders stepped down, and another one passed away. Two new elders from the congregation filled the void, one of which was an accountant. As one would expect of an accountant, he checked the books. How had money been spent? Were the bills current? Had anything been overlooked? Were the tithings current? Had one of the elders been dipping into the church funds for nonchurch purposes? The accountant knew that criminals often were members of a church, and possibly in his church.

When there is an audit, it is not uncommon for some discrepancies to be discovered. Usually, the discrepancies are minor, and the fix is quick and simple. Skullduggery is rare, but one never knows until the audit has been completed. Fortunately, Bernie Madoff and Samuel Bankman-Fried were not members of this church.

The new elder, Mr. Green Eye Shade, finished his audit. Something wasn't right. Something was missing in the last few years. He couldn't put his finger on it so he decided to do a quick check going back five years. Maybe he'd uncover whatever it was that was troubling him.

The search of the archives paid off—the pension fund! The contributions to the widow's pension were three years in arrears!

Mr. Green Eye Shade called a meeting of the elders and informed them of the problem. The church bank account was flush, but not so flush that it could pay three years of unpaid contributions. They could inform the congregation at the next service—not a good idea. They couldn't just ignore the problem until the little old widow finally retired and then say, "Ooopsieee!" Ignoring the problem was totally unacceptable.

The elders wisely decided to confront the truth and seek a solution by approaching several of the church's more affluent members. They did so, and the affluent members looked at each other, had a brief discussion among themselves, reached for their checkbooks, and wrote some checks to the church, specifying the pension fund.

Lessons Learned: The elders discussed and investigated the case of the "Great Pension Fund Ooopsieee." They concluded that there was no malfeasance, just that someone in the past had accidently dropped the ball. The elders agreed that they were fortunate that Mr. Green Eye Shade had discovered the oversight.

That is one of the functions of the elders—to provide oversight and manage the operation of the church. The elders did their job.

SUMMARY

This was a short chapter. Some vignettes are suitable to be in multiple chapters. You, the reader, probably saw the possibility with "Financial Wisdom" and "Steeple Chase." You'll see it again in the next chapter's vignette, "Cell Phone Tower." Finance is an area where the elders and clergy need to gather all the facts, and check the facts, before acting.

Rev. Stu Fud Shertz had his own ideas of how to spend money, especially the church's money. In his personal life, I'm sure he didn't spend money he didn't have.

Mr. Green Eye Shade used his accounting expertise to assure church funds were being spent wisely. He audited the books to confirm skullduggery hadn't crept into the church. Although he didn't find evidence of nefariousness, he did find an oopsie.

The church elder's work is never done.

— 7 —

CHURCH COMMUNICATION

Church communication requires that everyone participates. Everyone includes staff, congregants, and nonchurch members who interface with the church. Examples include radio stations, newspapers, local businesses, vendors, other churches, etc.

Churches have a bureaucracy, just like the government and businesses. The bureaucracy, when designed and used properly, facilitates communication within and outside the organization. Back in chapter 2, I showed the communication failure of President Kennedy regarding the Bay of Pigs and the communication success of President Johnson's staff meetings.

Weekly staff meetings are rather common in most organizations. Way back in the prior century, when I was in the air force, the base commander had a stand-up staff meeting every morning. *Stand-up* means everyone remained standing. Each staff member was asked to state in one or two sentences what they had planned for the day and any particular problem they faced. Problems were discussed and solutions, or a path to a solution, were resolved during that meeting. The meetings were designed to be completed in less than fifteen minutes. The result was everyone knew what everyone was doing that morning, problems were addressed at the highest levels, and things went smoothly for the rest of the day—usually. Don't forget Satan was always present helping Murphy's law to suddenly appear and create havoc.

Think *communication* as you read the vignettes in this chapter.

CANDLELIGHT SERVICE

The law of unintended consequences is always waiting to remind its transgressors who is really in charge. Another explanation is that Murphy's law is always lurking around the corner, excitedly anticipating the opportunity to prove its axiom "If anything can go wrong, it will."

Remember communication is paramount!

Things go well when there is full communication between all parties that are participating in a church service. A church service has a lot of moving parts that must be coordinated. A rehearsal of some kind absolutely helps if a service is going to do something different. Go into the sanctuary and walk through the service with all the involved parties.

A now senior clergy related the following experience to me. In retrospect, he finds it humorous. At the time, however, it really raised his pulse rate.

> I was a new assistant clergy at the church, and the senior clergy decided to have candlelight Christmas Eve services. However, the ushers hadn't been informed, and at the 5:00 p.m. service, the candles had not been brought out, nor had fire precautions, such as blankets, sand,

etc. This resulted in the ushers running around to find the necessary items to pull off the service.

The midnight service came off without a hitch; the 5:00 service had served as the practice service.

Church management had an oopsie and recovered. If there had been a fire, things could have been quite different.

Lessons Learned: Communication is vital. Transparency is vital. Everyone needs to know what everyone else is doing. Plan for the unexpected.

EASTER PARADE

Rev. Aye Won Fackts received a scathing letter of complaint from a congregant who had left the church. She complained that the choir director wouldn't let her sing a solo because she wasn't part of the *in* crowd. Rev. Fackts met with the choir director to get an explanation.

The choir director confirmed that the lady had asked to sing a solo. The director had said, "Fine, bring your music and we'll meet forty-five minutes before the next choir rehearsal." The member was a no-show. The next week, the arrangement was made again. The director said, "Show up forty-five minutes early, and we'll go over the music." Again, a no-show.

The complainer's attendance had always been spotty, and as later related to the clergy, it was discovered that the complainer wanted to sing "Easter Parade" at a service the week before Christmas.

Rev. Fackts thanked the choir director; case dismissed. This was a situation handled quite well, as are most complaints received by the vast majority of clergy. Church management worked very well.

Lessons Learned: There are always multiple sides to every story. To paraphrase Dan Crenshaw, a retired US Navy SEAL, in his book *Fortitude,* "Don't react quickly to information presented as factual. Gather all the facts before acting. Verify the facts. Be skeptical; consider alternate possibilities."

The news media—newspapers, radio, and television—all want to be the first to break a story. Some are so anxious to be first that they sometimes present false information as factual. Unfortunately, some of the media create news stories out of thin air to support their individual biases or in an effort to be the *firstus with the mostus.* The result is they lose the trust of their viewers and subscribers. Some current polls rate the news media trustworthiness as very low.

CELL PHONE TOWERS

This is an interesting vignette. A significant regular cash infusion to the church was rejected. A telecommunications company approached the church and asked if they could install a cell phone tower on the church property. Whether it would have been a standalone tower or hidden in the belfry was not revealed. The church elders replied very emphatically that they did *not* want that cell phone contraption on church property. It didn't matter how much the company was going to pay them. It was a no-way-Jose position. The elders provided no reason for rejecting the offer.

> Note: The rent payment to the church would have been $1,000 to $2,000 per month. This could have been the equivalent of ten to forty new families joining the church.

So the cell phone company installed the equipment on private property immediately adjacent to the church. Incidentally, the private property immediately adjacent to the church was owned by a member of the church—not a church elder.

Some speculation as to the reason for the rejection included the following:

* The close proximity to the cell phone tower causes cancer. Whether true or false, that certainly could have been an issue. And a very small number of people are adversely affected by being too close to power lines, radio transmitters, or even the electrical fields in their homes.
* One of the elders was a spellbinder orator and swayed the other members of the church elders to vote no. A good possibility, but it doesn't provide the reason why.
* The elders didn't want the church to be beholden in any way to the telecommunication company. Possible, but it doesn't sound logical. However, emotions, even if they have no basis in fact, can often cloud logic and the truth.
* The property owner maneuvered the elders to vote no so he could collect the monthly rent instead. Although I doubt it, it is a very real possibility. Remember money talks.

The congregation was not asked for their opinion. The story about the cell phone tower became known after the elders had rejected the offer. And as one would expect, a number of the congregants were displeased with the decision of the elders.

Lessons Learned: With the rearview mirror of hindsight, it would have been quite prudent to let the congregation know about the offer. The congregation could have provided a range of opinions both for and against the cell phone tower. In the end, however, everyone would have had the opportunity to express their opinion. The assorted rumors as to why the elders said no wouldn't exist. The open discussion and presentation of proposals could have resulted in the best decision. And that decision could have been for or against the cell phone tower. Hidden decisions almost always result in more discord and besmirching than open decisions with all the pros and cons being presented. The elders failed to communicate with their congregation. Remember the "General Manager" vignette in chapter 3.

STRIKE WHILE THE IRON IS HOT

The church search committee followed the diocesan protocol of asking for résumés, reviewing them, receiving diocesan approval, making phone calls, and interviewing candidates. Then they called to hire the best candidate.

Unfortunately, when they called the best candidate, they were informed, "Sorry, search committee, I accepted a position at my new church last month. You should have called sooner."

The search committee received the same response from the other suitable candidates.

Back to the beginning. Start the process all over again. Collect résumés, review résumés, obtain diocesan approval, call candidates, and interview candidates. Then, once again, select the best candidate and offer them the position.

It was the phonograph record with the same scratch that resulted in the same disappointing message. "Sorry, search committee. I accepted a position at my new church last month. You should have called sooner."

For the more youthful readers, a scratch on a phonograph record is similar to a "do-loop" in a computer program. Something just keeps repeating. (Sorry, you should have called sooner.)

The phonograph record scratch repeated when they called other diocesan approved candidates from the screening process.

What's a disappointed search committee to do? Well, they thought of something. They asked the bishop if they could ask for an exception to the selection process rules. The bishop granted them permission to shorten the process.

The committee started the résumé collection process again. Then the proverbial bolt from the blue struck; it looked like the ideal candidate. They sent the résumé of their ideal candidate to the bishop. The bishop examined the résumé, and I presume probably made a few discreet phone calls. The bishop called the search committee. "Yes, interview him, and if you still believe he's the right candidate, offer him the position of senior clergy."

The committee brought the candidate in for an interview, asked questions, got the answers they sought, and immediately made the offer. The candidate accepted.

Everyone was happy. The bishop was happy. The diocese had vetted the candidate. The candidate was happy—a shorter job search. The committee was happy. They had a senior clergy. The congregation was happy. At last, they had a permanent clergy.

Lessons Learned: Decades ago, there was an abundance of clergy, more clergy than there were positions. Starting in the late twentieth century, and so far in the early twenty-first century, that is no longer the case. Most denominations have a shortage of clergy.

The bishop and diocese review and approval of candidates was quite logical in a time of clergy surplus. The bishop wanted to assure that the best clergy filled the churches in the diocese. The rule was excellent when it was made.

The pendulum has now swung in the other direction. Now with a shortage of clergy, that means there is a shortage of clergy suitable to each individual church. The search committee wants the ideal candidate, an excellent candidate. They do not want just a suitable candidate or just a that'll-do candidate. They need to strike while the iron is hot.

The bishop realized that the rule as written was no longer suitable; times had changed. The bishop changed the rules and guidance to adjust to the changing times. The bishop delegated some of the decisions down to the church committee. The result was a win-win for everyone.

MOVING THE ALTAR

The following example may appear to be the proverbial mountain versus a molehill, but it illustrates what can go wrong, even when everyone is trying to a good job.

Decades ago, the elders and the clergy of a small church agreed to move the altar away from the wall. Previously, the clergy's back was to the congregation during part of the Eucharist (communion). After the altar was moved, the clergy would be facing the congregation during the entire eucharistic portion of the service. The congregation had been told the move would occur *after* next Sunday's service.

Next Sunday arrived and the elders were examining the altar early that morning and realized it would be a very simple move. So they moved it *before* the service. Some congregants were greatly disturbed because they were looking forward to the last service before the altar was moved. The location of the altar was an important tradition to them. Most members of the congregation were oblivious to the location of the altar. It's important to remember, however, that everyone views each change differently.

Lessons Learned: Communication failed. The congregation was expecting the altar to be moved *after* the service. While most of the congregation was neutral regarding the relocation of the of altar, some were not! While the elders did not intend to upset those congregants who were looking forward to the last service with the old altar location, they succeeded in upsetting them. The elders changed what they had communicated to the congregation.

Prevent as many conflicts as possible ahead of time. To use the cliché from the old Western movies, "Head 'em off at the pass!"

SUMMARY

This summary has a mini-vignette not about a church.

Many decades ago, I was at student at Fresno State College. I played in the band that performed at the college's football games. A lot of communication and coordination was involved. The band played a pregame show on the field, then returned to the stands. The band left the stands halfway through the second quarter and assembled at the back of the end zone—well away from the young men in helmets throwing a football through the air, chasing each other, and attempting to tackle the poor lad on the opposing team carrying the ball.

During one game, near the end of the second quarter, the man carrying the football was being pursued by a large number of men from the opposing team. The ball carrier was running as if critters from Satan's furnace were chasing him. He ran under the goal post and couldn't stop in time to avoid running into the band. A young lady held her flute up high as she was pushed into the band members behind her and screamed, "Not my flute!"

Unfortunately, the flute was damaged and needed a trip to the repair shop. Coordination with the repair shop resulted in a quick turnaround.

After halftime, the band returned to the stands. Those band members desiring a break were limited to only a few at any one time. The rest of the band played for touchdowns and bad calls by the referees. This was coordination between the band members the band director.

The whole evening of football couldn't have happened without the coordination and communication between the football coach, the band director, and scores of other individuals. The next time you attend a high school or college football game, think about the amount of coordination and communication required to present a successful evening of entertainment. That same amount of communication and coordination is necessary for a successful church service.

— 8 —

LOYALTY

A church consists of small groups, ministries, and individuals who come together weekly to worship as a group.

Loyalty has many different shades of definition and applicability. For example, a sports team (football, baseball, basketball, soccer, etc.) often feel a very strong loyalty to their leaders and teammates. These small groups of people work closely together as a team in practice as well as in games. When a fight breaks out and the benches clear, players come out to defend their fellow teammate(s).

The same is true for a military squad or platoon. The usual size of an army squad is five to ten, and a platoon is thirty. The greatest loyalty is to that small unit, then to the larger unit and the army. As is recognized in combat, the greatest loyalty is to the immediate squad and platoon. Yes, there is also a loyalty to the entire military and to their country.

As relates to a church congregation, it can be defined as loyalty to a leader and/or a ministry. In a church, the average size of a praise band is four to ten, although some praise bands can be much larger. Choirs range from quite small (three or four members), depending on the church, to a mega choir. These music groups function as a team. As such, they have a great loyalty to their own ministry, their fellow musicians, and their leaders.

LEADERSHIP

Leadership requires guiding a group; it also requires the ability to lead. An army colonel explained to me that one definition of leadership is motivating subordinates to do well because that is the right thing to do. Asking a subordinate to willingly do something they don't want to do, such as placing their lives in imminent danger. Successful leadership is based on trust, sharing information, and obtaining feedback (both positive and negative) from subordinates and team members.

Management is the controlling and directing of events. It involves allocating supplies or directing people to achieve a specific outcome. Management is often associated with budget, production of widgets, coordinating an organization's calendar, and management of resources (including people). It is often improperly equated with leadership. Management is often a part of leadership. However, leadership is not always part of management.

The fire department manages putting out a fire. The arson detective displays leadership in tracking down the arsonist and stopping the fires.

The first-grade teacher manages the classroom while teaching the children the alphabet. The first-grade teacher shows leadership when he or she determines that a specific student has trouble learning because of a hearing or vision problem.

Leadership usually involves removing the cause of a problem. Management usually involves fixing the results of a problem.

Depending on the situation, successful management can be

achieved without input from members of the team. Wherever possible, successful managers may also be leaders who obtain input from their team members.

Years ago, a navy admiral said that we don't need TQM (total quality management); we need TQL (total quality leadership). He defined the difference between leadership and management. Quality leadership usually produces quality results.

Keep loyalty, leadership, and management descriptions in mind as you read the following vignettes.

MUSIC GROUP IS TOO LARGE

Rev. I. M. Gawd was thrilled with just being assigned to the church. At last, he was fully in control of a church, one of his lifelong objectives. His rise to bishop would be next, he thought. He had told the selectors that he really liked contemporary music services. As would be expected, he began meeting with the leaders of the church's ministries.

After a few weeks in his position as senior clergy, he met with the music leaders of the contemporary service. He nervously looked at his watch and engaged in small talk. After several minutes, he announced that the contemporary music group was too large and to have the weaker members sit with the congregation. Whereupon he immediately stood up, said he had another meeting to go to, and walked out. In reality, he went home. The music leaders were not afforded the opportunity to explain that attendance varied and that the volunteer group was a ministry, not a group of paid professionals.

Rev. I. M. Gawd failed to understand that the group was a ministry to its members as well as to the church.

Lessons Learned: Rev. Gawd failed (refused) to hear a response to his request to downsize. Without feedback, he made a unilateral decision. Keep this in mind with this follow-on vignette.

MUSIC LOYALTY

Rev. I. M. Gawd asked to meet with the contemporary music leader in the summer after he had been at the church eight months. At the meeting, he informed the music leader that the coming year there would only be eight contemporary services, instead of the usual twenty. Furthermore, the twenty-member group was too large. Beginning that fall, there were to be only one or two guitars and a couple of vocalists. During the brief meeting, every time the music leader tried to respond, Rev. Gawd put his hand up in the face of the music leader and stated, "I am firm on this."

The following week, the music leader sent a letter of resignation, and several days later, he informed the contemporary service's twenty members of his resignation. The result was that six of the members left the church for another denomination, six went to another church of the same denomination, two remained, and four decided that they had had enough of organized religion.

Coincidentally, the choir director of the church who had always been opposed to the contemporary service had encouraged Rev. Gawd to discontinue the contemporary service. It was later learned that he expected most of the twenty contemporary members to join his choir. He was shocked when none of them joined his traditional choir.

Neither Rev. Gawd nor the choir director understood small group loyalty. Both Rev. Gawd and the choir director saw their position as a job, not a calling. Further, Rev. I. M. Gawd failed to understand how the group was part of the church culture and how it interfaced with the church as whole. This lack of understanding came home to roost when the annual church retreat schedule was being coordinated. The contemporary music group had been providing music at five different segments of the retreat for decades. Many of the congregation learned about the demise of the music group at the annual retreat. Now it no longer existed. Oops!

The old saying that you reap what you sow proved to be true for Rev. Gawd. Some congregants expressed their dissatisfaction with his destruction of the music group quite loudly in the presence of other congregants. After church services, Rev. Gawd would go the other way when he saw one of the congregants. He was avoiding another verbal chastisement for his shortsighted action.

Lessons Learned: The law of unintended consequences. Most ministries and groups are interconnected with each other. Remove one group, and another group suffers, including the congregants.

As stated previously, what are the downstream effects of the decision? If Rev. I. M. Gawd had met with the contemporary music group and the elders of the church before making his decision, he would have understood that the contemporary music group had become an integral part of the church culture.

GOODBYE, CHOIR

Rev. J. A. Kass was quite jealous of his very popular, and highly qualified, choir director. He continually made small, critical, and less than professional remarks regarding her during the service and in front of the congregation. Finally, having had enough, she resigned. The word of her resignation quickly spread throughout the community. A nearby church of the same denomination called her regarding a position. She responded, interviewed, and accepted the position as their music director. Incidentally, it was full time and included a significant pay increase. Almost the entire choir from her previous church voted with their feet and went to her new church.

Did the church elders let the reverend know what he was consciously or unconsciously doing? Perhaps the church elders did talk to the reverend and he failed to listen to them. Did the reverend really understand the dynamics of small group loyalty? Or did the reverend believe the choir's loyalty was exclusively to him? Did he dislike the fact that such a competent director was a lady? That's quite a few good questions and theories. We'll probably never know what the reverend J. A. Kass really was thinking.

Lessons Learned: Being mean rarely brings accolades to the one being mean. The man who's mean to his dog can't complain when his own dog bites him. When you're mean to someone, don't be surprised then they respond in kind.

A congregant of the choir director's previous church was asked what happened. Why did she leave? He thought for a minute and replied that the pastor lived up to his name: the cross between a horse and a donkey.

The next year, Rev. J. A. Kass was gone and a new clergy took over the church.

TOO MANY MINISTRIES

Rev. Aye Noa Behst was thrilled with his new position as senior clergy at the medium-sized church. He was especially thankful that he was no longer the clergy at a parochial school. While he hadn't fibbed on his résumé, he had shaded the facts just a teeny-weeny bit. Well, he admitted to himself, maybe just a little bit more than a teeny-weeny bit. But he had been truthful. He stated that he'd been the senior clergy at his last church for a month, which wasn't quite the whole truth. He'd been the on-site clergy for a month while the senior clergy was on medical leave.

At his new church, he looked at all the ministries; there were just too many of them. He thought, *People come to church for my sermons. All that is really needed are the flower folks, landscaping, building maintenance, choir, and office staff. Everything else is really just excess baggage that is a drain on my valuable time.*

Rev. Aye Noa Behst slowly eliminated a number of ministries. He even tried to eliminate a monthly dinner ministry. After all, he'd heard that the congregants talked about him at those monthly dinners. This ministry rotated couples from different groups to other couples' homes once a month to socialize. The congregants got to meet and visit with other congregants in depth, much more than was possible immediately after a church service.

The people, however, rebelled at the elimination of the dinner ministry and formed their own ad hoc ministry outside of the church and continued their monthly dinners.

Rev. Aye Noa Behst concluded that was just the way it was. At least he wouldn't be burdened by having to attend any more of those dinner meetings. He noticed a drop in attendance but rationalized that people come and go, so no big deal.

As I was writing this book, additional information came in. In three years, three of his assistant clergy left in the middle of the year. One left for a higher position in another state, one resigned midweek, and one gave notice the first of March that March was her last month.

Lessons Learned: This church has a problem, and the problem is most likely Rev. Aye Noa Behst. Rev. Behst failed to understand loyalty to ministries—loyalty to small groups. Coupled with the high turnover of assistant clergy, the probability of Rev. Behst being the problem is greatly increased.

SUMMARY

Loyalty is defined as faithful adherence to a person or group—duty or devotion to someone. A common example is a man's loyalty to his wife and a wife's devotion to her husband. Yeah, there's plenty of exceptions, but most husbands (and wives) will defend their spouse and family from bad guys with their life. And history is replete with one or two men coming to the defense of a single woman or child, even when the woman or child are complete strangers.

Rev. I. M. Gawd got into the management weeds with his contemporary music group. He believed it was too large and provided music at too many services, resulting in most of the members leaving that particular church.

Rev. J. A. Kass for some reason felt it was necessary to speak unkindly about his choir director during the church services. Then it was surprise, surprise, when the members of the music groups voted with their feet. A bond is formed when a small group works together; that bond is called loyalty.

Loyalty to a church ministry should never be ignored, underestimated, or misunderstood. The clergy's job is to lead the church, not to micromanage and insult the groups and leaders.

Loyalty, ability, and unsuitability arrive in the next chapter: IYI.

— 9 —
IYI

Smart people know what they can and can't do.
A few nonchurch stories to set the stage. Intelligent yet Ignorant (IYI)) individuals are present in every profession. IYI individuals are born without the full set of skills for some professions. They're not bad people; they just need to find their niche in life.

NETWORK ENGINEER?

This anecdote is from a network manager who experienced a unique personnel problem. There's nothing about a church in this vignette, but it is an excellent example of IYI.

The network engineer manager needed additional staff, someone to help manage his servers. An applicant had outstanding credentials. She was an honor student from an IT training academy. She had scored just about 100 percent on all of her tests. He called a teacher at the academy that he knew, who confirmed the woman's knowledge.

Her first day on the job, however, revealed a previously unknown shortcoming. She couldn't find the power switch on the server. As her short tenure progressed, it became apparent that she was a great book learner, an excellent memorizer, and a very good test taker. Unfortunately, her brain was not wired to solve problems. She was unable to make a practical application of the knowledge she held. She was an IYI.

Lessons Learned: The network engineer checked the applicant's references. She looked like an excellent choice. During the thirty-day probationary period, her unsuitability was discovered, and she was let go after two weeks.

A retired business executive related that hiring someone is a roll of the dice. A few new employees are stars, most are fair to very good, but a few turn out to be total misfits for the organization.

DELL COMPUTERS

This vignette is an excellent example of avoiding a management problem.

Michael Dell started making personal computers while he was still in college. His start-up company, PC's Limited, proved very successful, but he realized that his skill didn't include running a rapidly growing company. He hired an experienced CEO to come in and run it. He'd argue with the CEO, who would argue back and explain why particular business decisions needed to be made a certain way. Michael Dell was intelligent, but at the time, his best intelligence area was in computer building, not company leadership and management. His company grew so rapidly that he was not able to do the product development and manage the company at the same time. He recognized his time constraint and lack of management experience. He made a very wise business decision; he hired someone who could run his growing company.

Lessons Learned: The important lesson here is that he recognized his strengths, weaknesses, and limitations.

IYI

Nassim Taleb uses the term "intelligent yet ignorant" (IYI) to describe a certain type of book smart individual. Nassim Taleb is the bestselling author of *The Black Swan: The Impact of the Highly Improbable*.

The IYI term is applicable to those very few paper-qualified only clergy. IYI clergy were successful at seminary and are skilled at giving excellent sermons. However, when confronted with actually running an organization such as a large church (or even a small church), understanding the congregation, and leading its staff, they fail. They are unable to apply the seminary knowledge and become a successful religious leader. They may be better suited to a staff position; they are not suited to be senior clergy.

Think of IYI as you read the vignettes in this chapter. Just as some people are not destined to become professional basketball players, some are not destined to become a successful senior clergy.

ANTI-TEEN

Mrs. Mom and her teenage son were sitting in the back of the church when Rev. Fudy Dud Dee began his sermon. He stressed the unacceptability of many activities currently being enjoyed by teenagers. Skateboarding was a no-no, as was listening to popular music. Mrs. Mom looked at the teenagers in the pews in front of her as they slowly began slinking down in the pews. She later related that if she had been a teenager, she would have stood up and walked out of the service. Rev. Fudy Dud Dee continued and even criticized the time teenagers spent doing sports. Instead, they should spend that time doing community service projects.

Rev. Fudy Dud Dee was intelligent yet ignorant. He could give sermons, conduct religious services, and explain the Bible and the tenets of his denomination. Yet his brain was not wired in a manner that enabled him to utilize the knowledge he had acquired at seminary.

A few years later, Mrs. Mom reported that a new, younger clergy was heading the church. Rev. Dewit Rait reached out to the teenagers (tomorrow's church members), and overall attendance markedly increased, especially among the teenagers. He played soccer and basketball with the youth (like Bing Crosby in an old movie playing the role of a Catholic priest). The result was that the teenagers became more involved and helped with the thrift store and other church programs.

Lessons Learned: Rev. Dewit Rait understood and implemented church growth programs. He knew how to cultivate future congregations. Rev. Rait told the teens that whatever they could give was worthy. Rev. Rait was intelligent, and he was able to apply the knowledge he had acquired at seminary. He followed the love-them-into-the-church philosophy.

IDEAS

Rev. Breight I. Dias arrived at the very well-established church. The selection process had concluded that he was quite suited to this very large church with a congregation of over 5,000. The church had five services each Sunday, eight assistant clergy, three choirs, and a thirty-piece volunteer church orchestra.

The seven assistant clergy provided no-cost marriage and abuse counseling to the congregation as well as visitors to the church. Those outreach ministries were very effective in maintaining and growing church membership.

The exceptional quality of the choirs and orchestra attracted musicians from the community, which included musicians from other churches and other denominations. In essence, the church ministered to the community; it was a true cultural asset of the local area.

A church consists of its ministries that help make up the congregation as a whole. A church is greater than the sum of its parts, a real-life example of 2 + 2 = 5 (and that is *not* Ponzi scheme math).

Rev. Breight I. Dias settled in and realized that the church was quite healthy financially. However, there were some things that weren't broken that he thought needed fixin'.

Cut the assistant clergy. "Who needs all those assistants after all? I give the sermons." So he started laying off most of the assistant clergy. If congregants need counseling, there were professional shrinks and counselors to provide that service.

Cut the church orchestra. The clergy running the music program knew his time was running out, so he found a position in another church, which also happened to be in another state.

Mrs. Breight I. Dias had her untouched copy of Dale Carnegie's *How to Win Friends and Influence People*. It would remain in mint condition. When talking about the choir and orchestra, she referred to them as servants. And not just servants. She referred to the servants derogatorily; she would subtly spit the word "servants" when she spoke.

In two years, the church membership shrank from 5,000 to 1,500. Rev. and Mrs. Breight I. Dias couldn't understand why. After all, he had been to seminary and believed he had been anointed as flawless. Rev. Breight I. Dias was an IYI clergy. He was intelligent, acquired knowledge, and scored high in his classes at seminary. But he lacked the ability to apply the knowledge he'd acquired. I use the word *acquired* rather than *learned*. His brain wasn't wired to use the knowledge he had acquired at seminary.

Lessons Learned: I discussed Rev. Breight I. Dias's decisions with a friend who is a minister. She said one of the first things she was taught at seminary was "If it ain't broke, don't fix it." I expect that philosophy is consistent with seminaries of most denominations. Rev. Breight I. Dias must have been absent the day that was taught at his seminary.

CASUAL DESTRUCTION

It ain't broke, so I'm going to fix it. Rev. Idee Ten Tee arrived at the well-established church. He was very impressed with himself, very impressed that he had been selected for this prestigious church. He had a number of excellent ideas that he was going to implement.

One of the ideas had been percolating in the back of his mind for several years. The 11:00 service was a bit stuffy, what with all those suits and ties—those fancy Sunday-go-to-meeting clothes. He was going to relax that service. So effective next month, the 11:00 service would be held in the social hall. The dress was to be casual. There were to be no suits, no ties, no gloves for the ladies, etc. It was to be a dress-down service, a casual service. Think of it as the church equivalent of casual Friday at the workplace.

The service was casual, and in a few weeks, the church attendance had casually dropped rather dramatically.

Lessons Learned: Rev. Idee Ten Tee didn't follow the "If it ain't broke, don't fix it" rule. An after-the-fact question is this: why didn't he create a casual service at a new time? Where were the church elders when this decision was made?

Rev. Idee Ten Tee should have had a meeting with the elders and his staff. If he had done so, it's quite likely he would have scheduled the casual service in a new time slot. It could have attracted new members from the community. It could have been a win-win situation, not the lose-lose situation he created by acting alone. Remember to communicate and coordinate, get all the facts, hear the pros and cons, and then make a decision. The decision may prove faulty, but the faulty decisions will be fewer.

TOO MANY MINISTRIES—AGAIN

Rev. Mike Croman Ager arrived at his new church. He observed and he listened. He had seen ministries go rogue when he was an assistant clergy at his last church. He was determined that there would be no rogue ministries at his new church. He slowly implemented his program of having all the ministries report directly to him. He would manage all of the ministries. That would keep them corralled. They couldn't go rogue.

After a few months, Rev. Mike Croman Ager was becoming frustrated with all the ministries. There were just so many ministries. He carefully evaluated the purpose of the ministries and concluded that there were some unnecessary ministries. The solution, of course, was to shut down the ministries that he felt were of questionable value or perhaps outdated. Some had even outlived their usefulness or were in his opinion marginally effective.

Each Sunday, the reverend looked at his shrinking congregation. He surveyed the congregation about his sermons, and they said they were quite good. If that was true, why was the congregation shrinking?

Unfortunately, many congregants who were in, or supported, the closed ministries lost a major way in which they participated and supported the church. Some stopped going to church; they felt that the church had kicked them out. Some went to another church of the same denomination with a ministry like the one they had enjoyed at their previous church. A few went to a different denomination that had the ministry they desired. Some simply stopped attending church—any church.

Lessons Learned: Rev. Mike Croman Ager failed to fully understand that a significant portion of the church (which is the congregation) consists of its ministries. Eliminating the ministries eliminated the way some members gave and participated in the church. He failed to have a pro and con discussion about each ministry with his staff—and the leaders of the ministries.

SUMMARY

Some people are attracted to a ministry of a particular church, even if that church is not their denomination. One mother, the wife of a clergyman, had her children participate in another denomination's church youth program. Her reason: that church had an outstanding youth program.

Musicians, both instrumentalists and vocalists, often participate in music programs at churches other than their own denomination. Some will change denominations or churches; others will act as adjunct members of the other church, split their time with their home church, or attend irregularly.

It is rare that one church can offer ministries to all. It is beneficial if every church offers numerous ministries that suit its congregation and can draw from the community at large.

A few clergy reach their level of incompetence and continue through their career at that level. The result is mediocre religious leadership, which usually results in a mediocre church experience, which is displayed in a mediocre church culture. Four of the vignettes in this chapter illustrated the IYI traits. Rev. Fudy Dud Dee, Rev. Breight I. Dias, Rev. Idee Ten Tee, and Rev. Mike Croman Ager were intelligent clergy. They were very book smart and did very well in regurgitating information—like the lady in "Network Engineer." Their common weakness was their inability to successfully apply what they learned in seminary. They didn't have the ability to understand people; they didn't understand their weaknesses. Michael Dell, Dell Computers, did understand his weakness; he didn't have management experience. He knew he needed help to run his rapidly growing company. He hired a CEO.

Laurence F. Peter expressed the issue in an equation that sums it up (no pun intended) quite well in his book *The Peter Principle*.

> Incompetence plus incompetence equals incompetence. (1969, page 107)

The clergy of a megachurch has a separate room for visitors just outside the sanctuary. The visitor reception room answers questions and has a staff member and a video message for the visitors, who are potential church members. The clergy's video tells visitors and newcomers to his church that if they don't see a ministry they want to join, ask about starting a ministry. He wants everyone in the church involved in a ministry. He understands what makes his church successful.

Many IYI's view their work/position as a job, not a calling. They all come together in the next chapter.

— 10 —

JOB OR CALLING

If you enjoy life's work, it's a calling, not a job. Some individuals find being a clergy a suitable profession and make it a nine to five, five days a week job. The vast majority, however, see it as a calling. Those who were called into the clergy want to help people, to minister to their flock. The called cover a spectrum of personalities, backgrounds, and interests. The called all have the desire to help people, albeit in different methods. There is no end of the shift in their lives. They usually depart their workplace (church) at the same time every day, but they will often stay if the need arises. They seldom work a forty-hour week. A sixty-hour week is not uncommon.

Those who see it as a job perceive it differently. They may equate it to an assembly line of repetitive tasks during their working hours. Their reward is a paycheck on a regular basis and the status symbol of being called "clergy."

The following section about Arlington National Cemetery is a very telling comparison of a job versus a calling.

ARLINGTON NATIONAL CEMETERY

Arlington National Cemetery has twenty-five to thirty interments a day. The interment ceremony is poignant. Once you've been to one, it is an experience indelibly imprinted into your memory.

The family and friends assemble at the Administration Building. During this period, friends, family, and the civilian clergy (and/or the military chaplain) intermingle, express condolences, stories, etc.

In this example, the deceased was an Air Force colonel. The family and friends assembled at the Administration Building and drove to a preselected point in the cemetery, called the Transfer Point.

At the Transfer Point, the civilian hearse and the procession of cars stopped. The casket was transferred to a horse-drawn caisson by the military honor guard and pallbearers, whose precision was truly outstanding.

Once transferred, it is quite common for some or all of the family members, friends, the military chaplain, and the civilian clergy to walk behind the caisson to the interment site.

As experienced by me, in this scenario, the civilian clergy intermingled with the family and friends at the Administration Building and then walked with the friends and family members behind the caisson to the interment site. The clergy talked with the family and guests at a reception afterward. This is by far the usual process. This clergy had a calling.

In another scenario, which I also experienced, the civilian clergy arrived at the last minute, remained in the funeral home limousine all the way to the interment site, and left immediately after the interment. It is important to note that this was the norm for this clergyman. He had a job, not a calling. He was once overheard saying, "If it wasn't for all those pesky parishioners, this would be a nice job."

Lessons Learned: If the clergy sees it as a job, you're probably better off not having him or her at your church.

STOCK MARKET

Rev. Wahl Street conducted the memorial service, gave a token appearance at the reception, and quickly left. The reverend explained that he had an important meeting to attend. A male member of the church wanted to ask him a quick question before he left. Rev. Wahl Street went upstairs to his office, apparently to change. The man waited at the bottom of the stairs, and waited, and waited some more.

Perhaps something had happened to the reverend. Could he have slipped, fallen, and become unconscious? Could he be having a stroke or a heart attack? Quite concerned, the man went up the stairs to check on the reverend, perhaps even to save his life.

The man opened the door, and there was the reverend, at his computer, doing online trading. Rev. Wahl Street was a stock market enthusiast, or a stock trading addict. The weekday memorial service apparently disrupted his stock market activity.

The man, of course, was quite displeased that the reverend had treated the members of his church, and the family of the deceased, so shabbily. The man was a true leader of the community. He sat on the board of several national businesses and was even an advisor to a government think tank. The man was not one to accept such shabby treatment quietly.

Well, as one would expect, there were words exchanged. The man, so I was told, used a vast number of unchurch like words in expressing his displeasure to the reverend. And his highly descriptive words were expressed quite loudly, to the horror, and delight, of the ladies and gentlemen who were at the reception downstairs.

Lessons Learned: Rev. Wahl Street could have been a bit more discreet. He could have said that he received a call just before the service and that he needed to go upstairs and take care of some financial matters. If he'd done that, his trading addiction might have gone unnoticed.

Many people have an avid interest in a particular area. Some have very strong urges bordering on an addiction. A few are addicted to alcohol. Some are addicted to nicotine and must have a cigarette or other tobacco product. Unfortunately, a few individuals are addicted to drugs. Some people are gambling addicts who keep many casinos in business.

The vast majority of people are invested in the stock market through a pension plan or other retirement program. These people are investors. Some people elect to manage their investments themselves. They buy and sell stocks and bonds, improving their net worth and building their nest egg for retirement.

Rev. Wahl Street, unfortunately, was addicted to personally managing his investments on a daily basis. He needed his fix. The need for a fix was so great that it interfered with his chosen profession—clergy.

Maybe he chose the wrong profession. He should have joined a brokerage firm instead of going to seminary.

I suspect the elders did not know about his addiction, although some probably did know that he had an avid interest in the stock market. After the reverend's unfortunate addiction became known, I was told some congregants urged the reverend to seek professional help.

SUMMARY

People develop and use only a few of their talents during their lifetime. However, each individual has three hundred to five hundred skills that they can develop and use at a high level, but they only do so with one or two—maybe three or four for some people. As an example, consider the lawyer who directs the church choir. That entails two skills: lawyer and music.

A talented actor played the role in a movie of a baseball player who got sent to Japan. The baseball manager who helped with the movie said the actor could have been a successful baseball player, if he had taken that career path. He didn't develop that particular skill. He remained on the acting career path.

You want men and women with the skill and talent to be successful in their chosen profession of clergy. In addition, you want an individual who has a passion and ability to be clergy. They should feel a calling to the profession. They need to see it not as a job but as a calling.

— 11 —

SELECTION

You don't always get what you think you're getting. Stated differently, what you think you see is not always reality.

I'll take a brief jaunt through railroads, education, and medicine before reaching churches. However, there is a real purpose for this side trip, which should become apparent.

RAILROADS

Clayton Christensen's book *Competing against Luck* takes a rearview mirror look of some significant industries. In hindsight, his observations are easily explainable and quite obvious. At the time, however, they were not so obvious.

Christensen refers to jobs to be done theory. Keep the jobs to be done in mind as you read about each industry or profession. Railroads is the first example.

> The railroads were in trouble ... because they assumed themselves to be in the railroad business rather than in the transportation business ... the railroads fell into the trap of letting the product

> define the market they were in, rather than the job customers were hiring them to do. (2016, page 182)

The railroads didn't fully understand what business they were in.

EDUCATION

In education, what is the job we expect teachers to do? I believe it is to educate and train our children. Think about the job we are asking our teachers when you read the following excerpt.

> It's all too easy ... for managers to start managing the numbers instead of the job. A great illustration of this is the way public schools teach so their students will pass the requisite tests because the government depends on schools hitting certain measured standards. (2016, page 184)

You may justifiably ask, "How will the teachers know if their students are learning if they don't test them?" The skilled teacher will teach the subject to the best of their ability and test the students on what they have been taught. The skilled teacher will stress learning the subject in depth so it can be useful to the student. But what about the under skilled teacher?

MEDICINE

> Or in medicine, consider how doctors often treat symptoms, rather than getting to the cause of the problem. (2016, page 184)

The doctors set our broken legs. And they give the patients crutches. Unless it's obvious, they probably won't realize that the patient has a vision problem that caused them to step in the giant hole and break their leg.

RELIGION

Keep the railroads, education, and medical professions in the forefront of your mind as you read the next excerpt, which is about religion. What is the job to be done by a church or synagogue?

> The Jobs to Be Done Theory explains why so many churches are struggling to keep their members. They have lost a sense for the jobs that arise in their member's lives, for which they might hire a church. (2016, page 231)

WHY PEOPLE GO TO CHURCH

I looked at some polls that asked people why they did, or did not, attend church. One poll ranked the sermon at the top; another placed it in around the middle. One poll listed music near the bottom, another had it near the top, and one didn't list it at all.

How a question is asked has a big effect on the answer. A multiple-choice question steers the one being polled to a preselected answer. This makes percentages of predetermined topics very easy to calculate. The next time you receive a telephone poll, note how the pollster tries to steer you into specific answers—answers that may or may not precisely reflect your opinion. Think about the classic lawyer question of a man accused of beating his wife. "Are you still beating your wife? Answer yes or no." If you're a single man, you can't answer that question because you're not married.

If you're married and have never beat your wife, you can't honestly answer the question. The question doesn't apply to you.

Fill-in-the-blank questions expand the number of possible answers and provide a better answer to the poll. However, it is more difficult to provide neat little percentage answers.

So why do people go to church? What is the product, or outcome, people are seeking when they go to a church? Churches will place greater importance and emphasis in some areas based on their particular denomination, as well as each individual church culture. I like the bullet format. The following list I assembled after researching and talking to a number of clergy and nonclergy as to why people go to church. The reasons I've listed are not in order of importance. You, the reader, can probably list additional reasons.

* Spiritual growth and guidance.
* Social aspects, friendships.
* To feel a part of this church.
* The church is part of the community.
* Worship.
* Sermons.
* Music.
* Make me a better person.
* Clergy emulate God.
* The clergy is a model for me to emulate.
* The church and the congregation have mores and a culture similar to mine.
* Ethical and moral compass check keeps me going in the right direction—like seeing a police car reminds me not to speed.
* Contemporary services.
* Traditional services.

* Helping others in time of need.
* Worship style.
* Ministries (Bible study, youth groups, choirs, praise bands, etc.). Much of the church is comprised of small groups and ministries coming together to worship once a week.
* Church stability. Long-term clergy who maintain each individual church's culture. This is the opposite of short-term clergy (i.e., a new clergy every few years).
* Short-term clergy. New clergy every few years gets us exposed to new sermons and different interpretations of the Bible and encourages new and fresh ministries.

Rick Warren, in his book *The Purpose-Driven Church,* surveyed the members of his Saddleback Church in California.

> Of the church members surveyed 89 percent said, "The church's purpose is to take care of my family's and my needs." (1995, page 82)

After reading Clayton M. Christensen's book *Competing against Luck* and deducing what I believe to be his logic, people go to church because it is "what causes what to happen" (2016, page 231).

The church should be a factor in people's lives that helps cause good things to happen. The building, the music, the sermon, the stained glass, and social events are all important factors. But the core item is what the clergy is supposed to achieve. The clergy is the *what* that causes *what* to happen. This should be the primary focus and core of the clergy's job description.

CLERGY JOB DESCRIPTION

Rick Warren in his book *The Purpose-Driven Church*, states, "Every church operates in a unique cultural setting" (1995, page 67).

In a city with several churches of the same denomination, each will have evolved a culture that has a few unique characteristics. One of those churches will probably have a strength that really sets it apart from the other churches.

The clergy selector, whether a group at the church or an individual at the diocesan level, really needs to know in detail everything about the church's culture. The selector needs to know every ministry with a full description of its mission and how it fits into that church. Some may appear to be obvious, such as the flower guild, ushers, etc. However, the tasks performed, for example, by the ushers will probably have small differences at each of the churches.

The objective is to achieve an excellent match in which the congregation and the new clergy are very well-suited to each other. The differences should be known up front, and both parties need to reach a decision to achieve a win-win situation. It needs to be a perfect marriage of clergy and church, or at least a very good one.

> For the husband is the head of the wife just as Christ is the head of the church, the body of which he is the Savior. (Ephesians 5:23)

The vast majority of clergy strive to be a good match for a congregation. The church elders need to be very specific about defining their areas of responsibility and the clergy's areas. Everyone needs to agree beforehand that all changes, no matter how minor, will be discussed prior to their implementation. Remember the candlelight service earlier?

SUMMARY

What is your business? The railroads thought they were in the railroad business, not the transportation business. Is the purpose of education to teach to the test or imbue the student with a depth of knowledge that prepares them for life? Is the function of medicine to fix an ouchy or to find and cure the root cause of the ouchy? In reality each profession must fill both roles, not just the obvious role.

What is the business of religion? It is more than giving sermons; it's very encompassing in taking care of and improving the lives of the congregation.

It's doubtful that a vegetarian lady would marry a cattle rancher. However, it was quite likely that a vegetarian lady would marry a vegetable farmer or vegetable wholesaler.

This same initial screening is needed when selecting clergy, music directors, and elders. Do you really want a rap artist leading a conservative choir at a traditional Sunday service?

That may sound ridiculous, but look at the clergy mismatches in some of the earlier vignettes. Some were that'll-do choices, a choice based on some deadline or a choice when the clergy had a hidden agenda to remake the church to fit his or her concept of the "perfect" church.

Additionally, some churches sign a multiyear contract with a new clergy before they start full time. I pose the following question: why?

Almost all organizations, businesses, and government agencies have an upfront clause that the new employee can be terminated within thirty days if found unsuitable. Unsuitability is determined by the employer, not the employee. Is there a reason that the profession of clergy needs to be handled so differently? I believe the unwritten policy is "We've always done it that way. And because we've always done it that way, we'll continue doing it that way."

— 12 —

CLEAR MY DESK

The objective, the goal, what you want to achieve is what it is all about. There may be many possible solutions and an assortment of possible paths to the objective.

CONSEQUENCES OF CLEAR MY DESK

When a clergy vacancy is filled by the diocese, the bureaucratic culture sometimes raises its ugly head. The selector has made the obvious matches: square pegs in square holes and round pegs in round holes. Now, however, the selector may be faced with fitting rectangular and triangular pegs into oval holes. This can be described as one or more of the following dilemmas:

* Too few clergy to fill too many slots.
* Too many clergy to fill too few slots.
* Too few good clergy to fill too many slots.
* Matches as directed by the bishop have caused problems.
* After filling the easy matches, the selector is now faced with the necessity of making assignments that are not quality matches.
* The deadline is near; assignments must be completed.

The bureaucratic culture, or mindset, now takes hold. The desire to meet a deadline becomes the objective rather than achieving the best possible solution. Thinking outside the box could be discouraged or may not rise to the forefront of the selector's mind. Such thinking may be discouraged by tradition or denominational policy.

The result can be bad for the individual church and congregation as well as for the clergy involved.

Depending upon the diocese and denomination, the options could include changing the deadline, postponing retirement of some clergy, clergy sharing, a short-term interim clergy, or a long-term interim clergy. The paramount priority is to find the right leader for each church.

Rick Warren describes the following five kinds of churches in his book *The Purpose-Driven Church*:

* Soul-winning church
* Experiencing-God church
* Family-reunion church
* Classroom church
* Social-conscience church

He stresses that some churches are a blend of these categories. What is most telling is when there is a mismatch of church and clergy.

> For example, if a family reunion church thinks they are calling a pastor to be their chaplain and they get an evangelist or a reformer, you can expect sparks to fly. That is a recipe for disaster! (1995, page 126)

He says it differently, but very descriptively, later when he says,

> Many church conflicts are caused by mismatched leaders. Placing the wrong type of leader in a church is like mismatching jumper cables on a car battery—sparks are guaranteed to fly. (1995, page 177)

This mismatch is what happened with Rev. Hoity Toity, Rev. Demigh Gawd, and quite a few other examples described earlier. Keep them in mind as you read the next vignette.

RUSH TO JUDGMENT

Even if the individual church has its own selection committee, they face many of the same issues that the diocese selector faces. The following is a story of one selection committee.

The interim clergy is old and his health is rapidly declining. The committee lets the interim's health create a false deadline.

Ten possible clergy passed the screening process. They were ranked in order. The committee starts calling them, in rank order. The top nine have already accepted a position elsewhere or won't be available soon enough. The false deadline looms over them. The committee feels pressured to make a decision quickly.

Number ten is available sooner, even though he barely met the desired qualifications. The committee concurs that he will not be a star. He certainly won't be a Billy Graham or a Dwight Moody. He won't be an equal to Adam Hamilton, Rick Warren, or Bill Hybel. However, that would be a very high bar for any candidate. The *deadline* continues to loom over the committee's head.

The committee concludes, "Let's get this over with. We've been on this search for the perfect candidate for over a year." At some point, the committee decides that perfect is the enemy of good enough—or adequate enough. So good enough, or adequate enough, will have to do. Number ten is certainly not an excellent choice, but he's really not completely unsuitable.

The committee proceeds, number ten arrives, and he becomes the new senior clergy for the church. All clergy make mistakes, stumble, and make bad decisions. Most clergy learn from their mistakes, make corrections, and move forward as new, improved, better than ever clergy. A very few are mismatched and move on to another church that is a better match.

Some have reached their level of incompetence and will remain at the church, causing suffering for themselves and for the church.

Mediocrity reigns supreme until the clergy departs for another position, dies, or the church dies. Everyone loses. No one is a winner.

The incompetent, or mismatched clergy, is why the selection process is so important. The vignettes have described how a bad match, an inexperienced clergy, a poor group of elders, or even worse, a clergy with a personality defect can damage a church. The worst, of course, is when the elders are the problem, as evidenced in the "Elders Gone Wild" vignette in the next chapter.

The elders and the congregation must support the clergy. They need to guide him and help him make good decisions. Leading a church is a team effort. The church should not accept a mismatched clergy. Help the mismatched clergy on their way as soon as possible. In most cases, that mismatched clergy will be quite suitable at another church.

Lessons Learned: The objective, the goal, is what it's all about. A solution is only one of many paths to the objective. If it is the rare clergy that is a severe mismatch, then the elders and the congregation must have the courage to take steps to remedy the problem as soon as possible.

SUMMARY

Go back a few pages to the "Consequences of Clear My Desk" vignette. Rick Warren talked about the sparks flying with a mismatch. Earlier vignettes describe the problems caused by a mismatch. What is worse is when the new clergy arrives with his or her own agenda, an agenda that conflicts with the church's agenda or culture.

Strive for the perfect, or near perfect, match. Do not be pressured to accept a mismatch because of a deadline. Think outside the box. In many situations, the church may be better off without a senior clergy than with a mismatched clergy.

— 13 —

EXTRAJUDICIALISTS

There has been an increase in violence toward churches. Is it because there is less respect for religion than there was in the 1800s? Is it because we no longer house loonies in state hospitals and instead release them on the street? Society is always changing and the quicker society successfully addresses the impact of the changes, the safer we'll be.

ARMED GUARDS

There's been an increase of loonies who like to run around shooting people. Schools, churches, and malls have become inviting targets. They're excellent targets because most of the occupants are unarmed; they can't shoot back.

There are strong feelings both for and against guns, and there is justification for both sides.

Churches are particularly vulnerable because they are usually considered gun-free zones. Each church should address their vulnerability, evaluate their situation, and decide how they wish to address the issue. What they should *not* do is procrastinate and kick the can down the road.

I talked with one of my former coworkers, and she said that the ushers at her church were armed. Further discussion revealed that the clergy didn't officially know, and the ushers didn't officially tell him. It was a modified version of "Don't ask. Don't tell."

Another church has an off-duty policeman in the narthex during the service. That church has had the policeman present at their services for years.

A church in the western United States became aware of extremely subtle threats from an adjacent landowner. That church resolved the problem by having some armed men sit in front of the church during the services. The men were members of the church and also just happened to be law enforcement—in civilian clothes. The presence of the men stopped the subtle comments from the disgruntled landowner. It later came out that the disgruntled landowner wanted to buy the land to expand his farm. When the land was sold to the church—for a higher price—he felt cheated. He believed that he should have been able to purchase the land at a very low price.

Across the pond: After a number of knife attacks in England, there was a brief discussion about limiting the size of knives one could possess. The knife size restriction fizzled.

Loonies who like to murder also use cars, trucks, poison, clubs, and bombs to kill and injure people. As I was doing an edit of this book, the news ran a live update on an individual with twisted neurons in his brain. Mr. Twisted Neurons had stolen a small plane and spent hours boring holes in the sky and was threatening to fly it into a Walmart store. He finally crash-landed the aircraft and was captured. He also got attention. For some individuals, negative attention is better than no attention. Reference a child acting out in school.

Why do they do such horrible things? Talk to one hundred

law enforcement, doctors, and "experts," and you'll get lots of different reasons.

My explanation: Satan is having fun.

Lessons Learned: Society will eventually come to grips with the loonies. Until then, each church should decide what they're going to do.

CHURCH ELDERS GONE WILD PREPARATION

Reality is not always what it appears to be. Keep that in mind as I present twelve mini vignettes about how facts are distorted, spun, fabricated, hidden, bullied, and corrupted to achieve a predetermined goal. The first is a legend that just won't go away—presuming it is no longer in existence.

The Knights Templar were a great organization in their day. The knights were a major player in the crusades of the tenth and eleventh centuries. The knights were officially disbanded seven hundred years ago. With myths, legends, and rumors, however, there are reports of their continued existence as a secret society. Do they still exist? I doubt it, but some people believe they still exist.

Vigilantes, as depicted in the movies about the Wild West. Vigilantes took matters into their own hands and administered swift mob justice—or administered what they believed was justice.

> "Don't confuse me with the facts. My mind is already made up with misinformation."

Kangaroo courts provide a mockery of justice, with the judge and jury usually comprised of those who "know" the accused is guilty. The accused is often denied the opportunity to present evidence in their defense, or evidence that is permitted to be presented is declared false. After all, it must be false because the members of the kangaroo court know the accused is guilty. Let's hurry up, get it over with, declare him guilty, and hang him.

Spellbinding orators of yesteryear captivated crowds and decided elections but have been somewhat overcome by the emergence of radio and television. Some examples of bad (evil) spellbinders include Adolf Hitler and Mussolini. Good religious examples include Dwight Moody and Billy Graham.

The spellbinder effect can be found in small groups, such as juries, board meetings, and yes, even church elders.

The "Union V" is the strategic placement of a few men in a labor union meeting (in the shape of a V). The V men stand up and shout in agreement with a predetermined issue or speaker, in order to give the appearance that the majority of the members agree. Those members who remain seated see people standing and shouting on their left, their right, in front, and in back of them. It appears that almost everyone supports the issue or speaker. The result is intense pressure for members to vote the way supported by the Union V.

Demonstrations for TV news is another example of how a very few individuals can appear to be a large group. Think of the close-up view on television news of a group of demonstrators. It appears like a large group. A view from another news station shows ten to fifteen people carrying signs and marching in a circle in front of the TV cameras.

Machine politics fills the bureaucracy with like-minded individuals, also called yes-men, who pressure citizens to support the machine. For example, "You didn't contribute to the machine in the last political campaign. I'm not sure when we'll be able to fix the sewage leak in front of your house."

The totalitarian state is the ultimate in machine politics. Winston Churchill's description in *Memoirs of the Second World War* is a superb example.

> It is part of the Communist doctrine and drillbook, laid down by Lenin himself, that Communists should aid all movements towards the Left and help into office weak Constitutional, Radical, or Socialist Governments. These they should undermine, and from their falling hands snatch absolute power, and found the Marxist State. (1959, page 95)

The important phrase here is "...help into office weak Constitutional, Radical ..." which creates the cadres of yes-men. Machine politics is not limited to political parties; it can also exist in any organization that has a small management group within it. This includes church elders.

Whisper campaigns are used for quiet, behind-the-scenes dissemination of falsehoods to achieve character assassination of an individual and are not uncommon in political campaigns.

> "Did you know candidate Jones is really a space alien in disguise?"

Often the victim does not learn about the lies for years. And of course, a few of the whisper campaigns achieve urban legend status.

The big lie technique tells a lie that includes some elements of truth. Continually tell the lie, and eventually many people will believe it. Hitler blamed everything on the "international Jewry" who he claimed controlled the United States, Britain, and Russia.

Furthermore, his newspapers and radio stations continually reported that the Jews were waging a war of extermination against Germany. Hitler was able to get a vast portion of the population to believe his big lie.

> A lie gets halfway around the world before the truth has a chance to get his pants on. (Winston Churchill)

The big lie technique works when a falsehood is shouted loudly, without rebuttal, for a significant period of time. Adolf Hitler successfully used the big lie technique. He said the international Jewry were the cause of Germany's problems.

Consultants are used for many reasons in the business world. The CEO of a small consulting firm provided his inside viewpoint of how consultants are used on occasion.

A company bigwig wants to justify an existing or future decision regarding one of his company's products. He hires a consultant to evaluate the pros and cons of the market and possibly make a recommendation. If the consultant fails to provide the desired answer, the consultant is thanked, paid, and the report is filed in the bigwig's bottom desk drawer.

Consultant number 2 is hired and may, or may not, be shown the previous consultant's report. Mr. Bigwig may explain that the previous consultant didn't completely provide the necessary information. Consultant number 2 asks more detailed questions about the desired research, in order to properly meet the purpose of the assignment.

Most consultants try to provide fair and nonbiased reports, with the pros and cons of their recommendations. Some provide very bland reports in warm, soft, pastel-toned, feel-good reports. They say nothing really bad and nothing really good.

Others provide very sharp, no-holds-barred reports with strong recommendations.

A few consultants read between the lines, listen to the tone of the bigwig's voice, so that they understand what the "perfect" report will conclude and recommend. Keep this consultant information in mind as you read "Church Elders Gone Wild" next in this chapter.

Complainers are people who want to do things; they want to accomplish something. Depending on the setting, their need to accomplish something may be so great that they are steered into accomplishing something bad rather than accomplishing nothing. Rick Warren identified it rather succinctly in *The Purpose-Driven Church* when he said,

> The biggest complainers in any church are usually committee members with nothing else to do. (1995, page 379)

Empty suit disease infects some individuals when they are in a position of power. They become all puffed up with their feeling of self-importance, and suddenly they believe they are smarter than those not in power. Look back at "School Name Change" in chapter 3. As said earlier, it becomes important to the empty suits that they accomplish something, anything, to leave their mark.

Wrap up: Allegedly, today's culture doesn't approve of secret societies dispensing extrajudicial decrees, vigilante justice, or kangaroo courts. Unfortunately, it *is* happening today. Despite it being distasteful to accept, methods such as whisper campaigns, the Union V, and the big lie continue to flourish when given the right circumstances.

Whether by planning through machine politics or by serendipity, everyone in an organization, or ministry, has the same philosophy, mores, and biases; they will often agree with each other on just about everything. This is good if the goal is to defeat the enemy hordes attacking the city gates.

However, when they identify anyone who disagrees with them as the enemy hordes attacking the city gates, we have the unfortunate result of groupthink. Keep in mind the empty suit, a complainer, a report-directed consultant, and the other methods described earlier in this chapter. The result is that the stage is being set for an unfortunate outcome. Keep all of these little cameos I just described in mind as you read the next vignette.

CHURCH ELDERS GONE WILD

Rev. Knott Sew Peasee was the senior clergy of a medium-sized church. He was well liked by the congregation, and in his four-year tenure, the church had increased its attendance and tithing. It appeared that everything was going well.

One of the church elders, a spellbinder who I'll call Ms. Unhappy, disliked the phrase on the church web site "Everyone is welcome." Ms. Unhappy didn't feel it was sufficiently inclusive. Her eleven-step program to achieve "inclusiveness" is enlightening.

Step 1: Ms. Unhappy met with the reverend and recommended that the web site be changed to read, "Everyone is welcome, including gay, lesbian, transgender, transracial, transspecies, transplanetarians, and even the not-so-sures." She continued. "Why, just the other day a man wanted to marry his laptop computer." Rev. Knott Sew Peasee disagreed. He felt the phrase "Everyone is welcome" said it all. Further, he stated that the church was a hospital for sinners and there was no need to go into such detail as that might discourage some folks from attending. Additionally, people come to worship, not to be labeled.

Step 2: Ms. Unhappy possessed a very strong personality, had an intimidating presence, and could be a real spellbinder when she got going. Ms. Unhappy discussed the matter with other like-minded and undecided elders. She convinced them that something needed to be done. Several weeks later, the elders held a meeting, without the reverend, to discuss the "Everyone is welcome" issue. Using persuasion, cajoling, spellbinding oratorio, as well as an assortment of other tactics to get the other elders to change their minds, Ms. Unhappy then scheduled another meeting with the reverend.

Step 3: At this point, all but one of the elders agreed with Ms. Unhappy, and that one was wavering under her brow beatings. At the meeting she had called, she demanded that the reverend change the web site and that he personally bless the unions of nontraditional couples. She informed the reverend that he was allotted only three minutes to respond. The reverend said no, he would not bless such unions, but that the assistant clergy had done so in the past and was quite willing to bless unions of nontraditional couples. Further, the diocese said it was the choice of each individual clergy whether they blessed nontraditional unions. The reverend said he was following the guidance of the diocese. So what was the problem?

That was not the answer Ms. Unhappy expected or desired. Back to the drawing board. Such resistance to Ms. Unhappy was not acceptable. She was going to make sure the necessary changes she wanted were made. In her mind, she was a representative of the congregation. In reality, she was not; she just had her own agenda.

Step 4: Ms. Unhappy took the position that if the facts don't support your position, change the facts. So she changed the facts.

Step 5: Ms. Unhappy hired a consultant and let him know in no uncertain terms what the problem was and what his report should say. The consultant knew the questions to ask, how to ask the questions, and who should be questioned. Ms. Unhappy got the manipulated report she desired. Facts were fabricated.

Step 6: Ms. Unhappy decided that she must call and inform the bishop of the findings. The bishop was told, in no uncertain terms, of the terrible reverend, declining attendance, and the financial straits that the congregation was facing in the near future. "Why, my dear bishop," she purred, "I even hired a consultant to evaluate the situation, and his report was not at all favorable about the reverend."

I suspect the bishop thanked her for being so thorough in her work and was relieved that he wouldn't have to take such action himself. Ms. Unhappy had already done the necessary dirty work; she would give the ultimatum to the terrible reverend. *If fate looks favorably upon the diocese,* thought the bishop, *that terrible reverend might leave clergy-hood, or at least the diocese.*

Step 7: Several weeks later, Ms. Unhappy called another meeting of the elders and the reverend. The reverend was informed that his pay was being cut 25 percent because tithing had decreased and attendance had dropped. (In reality, tithing and attendance had both increased. Recall the big lie technique and kangaroo court.)

The consultant's report confirmed that Rev. Knott Sew Peasee was not a good clergyman and that he was being tolerated by the congregation. (Change the facts.)

Step 8: Rev. Knott Sew Peasee called the diocese and asked what was going on. The bishop informed him not to rock the boat, look for another position, and tell the congregation that he had been called to another church. The reverend did so.

Step 9: With no support from the bishop and the elders believing Ms. Unhappy's misinformation (and refusing to listen to him—kangaroo court), Rev. Knott Sew Peasee realized it was time to leave.

Note: There was a shortage of clergy in his denomination.

Step 10: At his last service, Rev. Knott Sew Peasee informed the congregation of the elders' decision and that he had been called to another church. He also expressed sorrow over failing to meet the congregation's desires, as expressed to him by the elders.

The reverend stood up to the bully by telling the entire congregation exactly what the elders had said—true transparency. Bullies use intimidation, try to establish fear, and try to control the situation. Rev. Knott Sew Peasee called her bluff and exposed her for what she was. Rev. Knott Sew Peasee let the truth be known. In effect, he cut Ms. Unhappy off at the knees.

Step 11: The congregation was shocked that he was leaving as they were very pleased with his service and how he had grown the church.

Ms. Unhappy was shocked by the congregation's response. There were gasps, crying, and congregants from the pews asking him to reconsider and to stay. Ms. Unhappy realized that the congregation just didn't understand what a great service she had done for them. Didn't they realize that they should be rejoicing at her success in ridding the church of such a straightlaced traditional clergy? Ms. Unhappy's failure to win the support of the congregation shocked her.

That particular Sunday, everyone bypassed station communion (congregants receive communion standing up and receiving communion from lay leaders) and went directly to the altar to receive communion personally from Rev. Knott Sew Peasee.

At this point, Ms. Unhappy took the realistic position that discretion was the better point of valor and made herself unavailable for the rest of the day.

As a sergeant once explained to me, the facts eventually come out, and in a church, they usually come out mighty fast.

Step 12 (Bonus Step): The following week, a group of congregants called the diocese and asked for a meeting with the bishop. The bishop was pleased to oblige and came to the meeting. He discovered that the meeting was not what he expected. Ms. Unhappy had apparently given him bad information. The congregants were quite vocal in expressing their disappointment regarding the crude and unjust dismissal of their beloved reverend. The bishop had failed them.

Displeasure was expressed in very loud voices, often many voices at the same time, directed at the bishop. The bishop realized that everything was rapidly going to the great-down-below in a hand basket.

The score at this church was Satan = 1: Bishop = 0.

And the instigator, Ms. Unhappy, had failed to change the church.

Lessons Learned: Could, or should, Rev. Knott Sew Peasee have stayed and fought it out? Should he have left quietly? The reverend took the honest and straight forward approach. He announced the elders' decision and confronted their assertions head-on. With no support from the bishop, and the brainwashed elders against him, he made an excellent choice. It is unfortunate that the church was the biggest loser in this fracas. The reverend is now at a church that likes a traditional clergy.

Looking in the rearview mirror, it is rather easy to see where a number of course changes could have been made along this path to prevent the storm-swept church from being the proverbial ship crashing into the rocks. I offer five possibilities and comments.

1. After the first meeting with Ms. Unhappy, Rev. Knott Sew Peasee could have made an announcement at a Sunday service about the elders' suggestion and why he felt such a change would be divisive. However, such an announcement in itself could have been divisive. Rev. Knott Sew Peasee really didn't have any good options. He elected to take the no-action-at-the-present-time approach. With the information available at that time, it was certainly a good decision.
2. Early on, the bishop should have gone to church and had a meeting with the congregation and the reverend, where he would have discovered that such a change was not the wishes of the congregation. The bishop reacted to the fake and biased information given to him by Ms. Unhappy. He failed to gather all the facts and verify the facts before acting. The bishop failed leadership 101.
3. The bishop certainly waffled on his guidance that the blessing of nontraditional unions was the choice of each individual clergy. His leadership failure was quite visible when he abandoned Rev. Knott Sew Peasee. The bishop reacted to Ms. Unhappy's fabricated and biased report. As said in the previous paragraph, the bishop failed leadership 101.
4. The clergy selection process possibly failed. If the church was liberal, why hire a traditional clergy?
5. If the church was traditional, why elect such liberal elders?

Note 1: The bishop retired a few months later.
Note 2: One year later, weekly attendance had dropped from

150 to 102. The church was in the process of searching for a new senior clergy.

Note 3: Ms. Unhappy managed to arrange to be in charge of the search committee for a new senior clergy. The job description was vague. The ideal applicant should like potluck dinners, have a sense of humor, and enjoy sitting on the porch at church retreats. One former congregant said Ms. Unhappy wanted a golden retriever, not a clergy.

The end result of Ms. Unhappy's great campaign was a fractured church. Some congregants quickly departed to other churches in the area. Ms. Unhappy experienced a pyrrhic victory; she won the battle but lost the war. She was left holding an empty paper bag. It is unfortunate that Ms. Unhappy will probably never realize the truth about campaign she waged.

The following vignette shows a positive result of extrajudicial action. This didn't involve a kangaroo court, vigilantes, or a power-hungry congregant intoxicated by groupthink. But it does show a rather effective way of how to break the inertia often exhibited by a bureaucracy—in this case, a church bureaucracy.

REAL MEN

Rev. Ped E. Filest built a large and successful boys' choir. Members included children from his church as well as young boys in the community from other denominations. It was unfortunate that his interest in the young boys went beyond the marvelous music experience he had created for them. He started trying to give more "personalized" attention to some of the boys. Word quickly spread among the parents about his nonstandard attentions. A delegation of mothers went to the bishop and expressed their concern. The bishop was quite polite, expressed concern about what they told him, and said he would take the appropriate action.

Several weeks went by and nothing had been accomplished, although the bishop told the mothers that he was judiciously working to resolve the issue.

Finally, a group of fathers went to the bishop and said that if Rev. Ped E. Filest was still in town tomorrow, his well-being could no longer be assured. Rev. Ped E. Filest was out of town before the sun rose the next morning.

Lessons Learned: When proper action is taken, mountains can be moved and bureaucratic inertia can be quickly overcome.

Using that magic mirror of hindsight, a very good case could be made that the parents should have gone to the police. Perhaps they were influenced by their respect for the bishop and the church, or they didn't feel they had sufficient evidence to take to the civil authorities. The result is that the pedophile will be able to practice his abominable behavior elsewhere.

It is important to note that some denominations have a policy that bad clergy are the responsibility of each diocese. Bad clergy are *not* to be pushed off on another diocese. The problem clergy must remain with the diocese,

NEW CHURCH

It was a small-town suburb close to a large city. For reasons known unto themselves, some of the citizens decided that they wanted to start their own church. It would be a coffee house type church. Only one problem: they didn't have a clergy. That was a problem that some of the more affluent members of the group said they could fix.

A short time later, a house was identified. It would be the rectory/parsonage, the home for the clergy, when they found him or her.

And of course, they found a clergy who said yes: Rev. Know Ital. The members of the start-from-scratch church drafted a constitution (their term) and identified members to serve as elders.

"Whoa!" yelled Rev. Know Ital. "There are some items in your constitution that won't work. We have to change them. And the candidates you selected to serve as elders are too young and inexperienced. You don't have anyone smart enough to be an elder in my church. But don't worry. I'll serve as the elder as well as the clergy of this church. After all, I've been to seminary and that means I'm smart enough to do both jobs with both my hands tied behind my back."

Of course, this was not what the start-from-scratch church members anticipated or wanted. There were discussions, and probably some very loud discussions, with some rather unchurch-like words. Rev. Know Ital sat back and smiled. He had convinced the search committee that the parsonage should be in his name. That would show that the members trusted him and loved him.

Well, as to be expected, and probably designed by Rev. Know Ital, many of the start-from-scratch church members voted with their feet. The remaining members examined their miniscule numbers, looked at Rev. Know Ital's hand stuck out for his salary, and concluded the following:

1. We've been had.
2. Maybe this wasn't the right way to start a new church from scratch.
3. Maybe, just maybe, Satan is laughing at us as the reverend owns the house and we have nothing.

Lessons Learned: There was nothing wrong with the start-from-scratch church idea. The problems that arose were due to faulty planning. I expect the members were quite enthusiastic about starting their own church. Enthusiasm is a necessary ingredient for a new church. I suspect that early on, they neglected to have a brainstorming session about the church's constitution and the parsonage. That session, with everyone expressing the positives and negatives of each item of the constitution, could have prevented the demise of the church. And of course, the vetting process of selecting their clergy also apparently failed.

Historically, worship was two or more people who gathered together to worship. Additionally they jumped the gun in trying to get a clergy before the church had settled in with members serving as lay leaders.

And of course, it appears that Rev. Know Ital was just a greedy man looking to get a free house. Satan is probably still laughing about this fiasco.

Satan = 1: New church = 0.

SUMMARY

All it takes for Satan to win a battle or a skirmish is for the people to wait for someone else to take the necessary action—known as the let George do it syndrome. This is what happened when Ms. Unhappy started her multistep program to change the church. The other elders were successfully browbeaten and steamrolled by spellbinder Ms. Unhappy. The bishop reacted too quickly. He failed to gather all the facts before acting. And he failed to discuss the issue with Rev. Knott Sow Peasee, the elders, and the congregation before making his decision. The bishop failed in his role as bishop.

In the vignette "Real Men," the mothers confronted the bishop about Rev. Ped E. Filest. The bishop, however, failed to check and gather all the facts. Instead he instigated the bureaucratic brush-off often called the slow roll. One definition of slow roll is when a person seeking an answer is continually put off. Politicians are very adept at this.

By ignoring the issue, the bishop hoped the problem would go away; it didn't. The group of fathers really got the bishop's attention and the slow roll technique was quickly forgotten. Unfortunately, the bishop just shoved the problem off on someone else.

The start-from-scratch church members failed to pay attention to details. They put the proverbial cart at the wrong end of the horse when they told the horse to giddy-up. They didn't complete their constitution, which would (should) have defined the tenets of their church and what they wanted in a clergy. The result was that a good idea was destroyed, a new church failed to get started, and a corrupt clergy got a free house.

— 14 —

OUTSIDE THE BOX

Humans are creatures of habit. Once we learn how to use something, most of us continue to use the same tool for other tasks. Many women tend to use a pair of scissors, rather than a knife, to open a cardboard box. Scissors and bobby pins are tools that most women are familiar with. Most men tend to use pocketknives, hammers, and other hand tools.

Those individuals who are chronologically blessed may still stomp their left foot on the floor of the car to dim the headlights at night. Once learned, habits are well ingrained in our memory. However, it's important to be able to think *outside the box.*

THE GREAT BAPTISM

The Saturday contemporary service had a usual attendance of thirty to forty-five. This particular Saturday, however, there was going to be a baptism. Baptisms were usually held on Sunday mornings, but there were conflicts for the extended family. Saturday evening was finally agreed upon.

The music selected for the Saturday services usually related to the readings in the *Revised Common Lectionary*. For this service, however, the music was changed to be in keeping with a baptism.

Since the Saturday attendance was usually on the small side, there was no usher. The service was held in the social hall, in keeping with the informal atmosphere of the contemporary service at this church. Additionally, the custom was for the music director to be the first one up for communion, followed by the congregation seated in the front row. The front row would automatically follow the music director to the communion rail. After taking communion, the music director would return to the music group and direct them in suitable music for communion.

The service was going well. The actual attendance was around one hundred, mostly due to the extended family of the baby being baptized. And as fate would dictate, most of the extended family were not the same denomination as the parents of the baby. The structure of the service was unfamiliar to them.

As stated earlier, when the communion part of the service began, it was the custom for the music director to be the first to go for communion, followed by the congregation in the front row. That's where fate intervened and really tried to mess things up. The extended family was seated in the front row, and they just sat there waiting for the clergy to do something. The music director saw the look on the clergy's face and decided that being an usher was more important at that moment than being a music director. So he began ushering folks up to the communion rail.

A soprano (retired AF colonel) saw a leadership void—no pilot in the cockpit. She wisely decided that an untrained music director was better than no music director. She quickly moved behind the director's stand and started the twenty-piece music group.

The service finished without a hitch.

Lessons Learned: In hindsight, it would have been nice to appoint someone to serve as usher. The extended family was much larger than anticipated, which tossed the proverbial monkey wrench into the service. Fortunately, teamwork paid off. Everyone pitched in and did what was necessary for a successful service.

This type of teamwork is the norm in most houses of worship, and that's the way it's supposed to be.

ROOT CANAL

The music director, Mr. Bieg Noat, had a slight toothache. Well, as Saturday progressed, the toothache increased to a tooth-hurt, to a tooth-really-hurt, to a tooth-Armageddon. It was well after midnight when he called his friend, the church pianist, who took him to the emergency room. Once there, he waited, and waited, and waited. The emergency room functions on a first-come-first-served basis, as well as triaging—taking the most serious patients first.

After many hours waiting, his name was called at four in the morning. Then he was informed that he was in an emergency room, not a dental office. To relieve the pain, they gave him a shot of morphine and told him to see his dentist the next day.

Realizing he would be in no shape to direct the three services starting at 8:00 that morning, he called Sub Sam, a friend (of another denomination), to substitute for him. Sub Sam said yes.

Sub Sam emailed his church where he played an instrument with four other musicians in support of his church's twenty-five-voice choir. "I won't be there this morning; I'm substituting at another church."

He arrived at Bieg Noat's church at 7:15, met the pianist, and they planned out the morning. Sub Sam directed the choir at the 8:00, 9:00, and 11:00 services. Additionally, he played communion music on the piano for part of the 9:00 service while the pianist took communion.

Lessons Learned: Director Bieg Noat and Sub Sam thought that was the end of their little musical chair adventure. After all, the objective was to have seamless music at the three services. They felt it was similar to a neighbor being forced out their house due to a fire. The neighbor goes into your guest room for the night, maybe several nights, and you feed them. You don't charge them rent for lodging and meals. It was just something that one does.

Well, bureaucracies exist, even church bureaucracies. Many weeks later, Sub Sam received a check in the mail for his substitute services. He hadn't asked for payment, and Director Bieg Noat hadn't requested that payment be sent. Bieg Noat didn't even know about the payment until years later when Sub Sam told him about it.

Such musical support, and church-to-church support in other forms, occurs every day (be it a weekday, a Saturday, or a Sunday). That's the way it's supposed to be.

DID YOU ENJOY LUNCH?

The couple was new to the area, and they attended a storefront mission church of their denomination for the first time.

The service, which included communion, went well. After the service, they were greeted by the other members of the small church.

It is important to note that since it was a small mission church, there were no permanent fixtures or storage space. They were only renting the space for the Sunday morning service.

After the service, as was the custom at this getting started mission church, the lay readers and chalice bearers were offered, and told, to consume any leftover wine and wafers. Since the wine and wafers had been blessed (consecrated), they were *not* to be thrown in the trash. After the lay readers and bearers had consumed the unused sacraments, one elderly member of the fledging congregation asked them, "Did you enjoy lunch?"

Lessons Learned: Not too much to say here, but it's another case where everyone pitches in to make the service a success. And as stated in several other vignettes, that happens in churches every week, and that's the way it's supposed to be.

FOOTBALL

It was a small church, and the senior clergy and the elders knew the demographics of their congregation.

Some churches have rather affluent congregations, and others have rather poor congregations. Some have well-educated congregations, and some are comprised heavily of high school graduates and dropouts. This church's demographic mainstay was football. Football Sundays sprouted backyard BBQs, adult beverages, comfort food, and lots of fun.

The elders and senior clergy knew what to do. Their congregation asked for the Sunday service times to be adjusted on occasion, as necessary, to accommodate the football schedules.

The result was that some Sundays, the services were held earlier than usual. The time changes were necessary to accommodate the congregations football culture.

Lessons Learned: Not included in the story the individual related to me was whether the elders were also football fans. Based on the flexible service scheduling, I infer they, too, were football fans.

Many churches offer a 7:30 or 8:00 Sunday morning service

usually without music, which is often referred to as "Fisherman's Mass." Some churches refer to the early service as "Golfer's Mass." The title isn't that important. What is important is that the senior clergy and the church elders recognize the culture of their congregation and adapt to it. The same can be said for Saturday evening services. The service time is scheduled to meet the needs and desires of the congregation—as well as to attract new members.

This church adapted to the desires and needs of the congregation; that's the way it's supposed to be. They thought outside the box when scheduling.

CONGREGATIONAL MELDING

Most churches have social gatherings, dinners, picnics, retreats, post service get-togethers, etc.

This particular church had a custom of long-term foyer groups. Many churches have foyer groups; some require signing up, and a staff member assigns the couples, or singles, to the specific groups. This particular church got all the interested couples in a room together—in this case, eighty couples. They were instructed to establish groups of four couples; three-couple groups were OK, too. The guidance was that the group should consist of congregants who really didn't know each other beyond saying hello once a week at church.

When the groups were formed, there were brief discussions, and some last-minute switches were made. The guidance to the groups was to meet once a month for dinner—for a year. That's a total of twelve dinners. The dinner host for the month would identify and provide the main course. Next, they would contact the other couples and assign them what to bring: salad, side, or dessert.

The goal was that during the year, they would really get to

know each other. The couples would know each other beyond a once-a-week greeting at church. The following year, the process would be repeated, with new groups of four couples each who would have a year to really get to know each other. And yes, there also some three-couple groups.

Lessons Learned: I found the self-assigning one-year foyer group concept intriguing. This may be the norm for many churches, but it was a new concept to me. One church I attended had a once-a-month foyer group. A church staff member would call three couples, establish a date, and the senior clergy would join the couples for dinner. The next month, the staff member would call three other couples and repeat the process. They were meet-the-clergy dinners rather than get-to-know-your-fellow-church-member dinners.

This full-year foyer group concept that incorporates the entire congregation each month can really create a bond among the congregants. After the annual pairing-off session, it is up to each individual group to determine when, where, etc. It also enables a young couple who never hosts a dinner because their apartment is too small to still participate.

Additionally, one woman explained to me, "Now I can use my nice China and dining room table and entertain more often. Before, I would look at my nice dining room table, my lovely China, and realize I only used it at Thanksgiving."

THE GREAT COOKIE WALK

A chief financial officer of a manufacturing plant once told me that new ideas that save money, or time, are usually very small ones. Half a percent here, a percent there, a tiny fraction over there, etc. He said occasionally a significant breakthrough would provide a savings of 5 or 10 percent, but such breakthroughs are rare.

Fundraising ideas for churches are usually social events. Everyone comes in and buys or donates in some manner and the church collects money and everyone has a good time. The result is some money is collected for the church, usually a few hundred dollars. Sometimes more. And occasionally, quite a bit more.

I had a neighbor who ran her church's quarterly white elephant sale. Many of the neighbors, not of her denomination, gave their excess clothes, furniture, and other items to her. She said her church made an average of $2,500 at each quarterly sale.

Now to the "Cookie Walk" vignette.

Ms. Lora Lee had an interesting idea. She talked to a number of fellow women who concurred that it was a good idea. The church would sponsor a cookie walk. The social hall would be lined with tables. Each table would have large platters of each woman's favorite cookies. Men could bake cookies and participate, too.

Congregants could buy an empty small box for $5 or an empty medium box for $10. With the empty box, they could walk down the aisle of cookies and fill their box with the cookies they wanted. Well, the word spread. The word really spread. I mean it really spread—throughout the entire town. Word-of-mouth advertising really works. Lots of nonchurch members came with $5 and $10 bills in their hands. What was intended to be a small church fundraiser was highly successful. The cookies were sold out by 11:00 that morning—not 2:00 in the afternoon with leftovers as anticipated.

A total of $1,800 was raised, much more than expected. I suspect some Girl Scout Cookies may have been available, too.

Lessons Learned: Success often breeds success. At this church, the plan for the following year is to offer three sizes of boxes—small, medium, and large—with prices of $5, $10, and $15. And have more cookies—lots more cookies.

Discussions included moving the cookie tables onto the lawn

and maybe part of the parking lot as well as the social hall. Maybe they'll even have some Girl Scout Cookie tables. This was outside the box thinking.

SPECIAL HELPER

There are all types of people, and of course, all types of teachers. Teachers specialize—math, social studies, English, music, art, etc. Very few teachers train to be teachers of the visually impaired.

In this vignette, the mother is a teacher of the visually impaired. The mother also has a five-year-old daughter. Young daughters (sons too) usually know something about what their parents do. Is Mommy a policewoman, an airline pilot, a teacher, a nurse, a stay-at-home-mom, a business owner, a doctor, etc.?

Now it's summer. Its vacation Bible school time of the year. The theme this summer includes a reenactment of the Bible story of Jesus restoring sight to a blind man. Mother, of course, sees a potential problem. She was concerned that her daughter wouldn't understand the symbolism of the story and would misinterpret it as blind people needed to be healed—that there was something wrong with being blind. Mom couldn't heal blindness. Additionally, medicine hasn't advanced enough to heal many forms of blindness.

The mother knew her daughter wouldn't understand that some blind people couldn't be cured and had to learn to live with their sightlessness.

A solution, of course, would be to change the program to delete the reenactment of Jesus restoring sight to the blind man. Mom discussed the issue with the clergy, who nodded knowingly, and said she would look into the matter.

The clergy talked to the vacation Bible school organizer. Unfortunately, the organizer evaluated the program and concluded that as written, it wouldn't work very well if that story were eliminated. While that particular story might be unsettling for the mother's daughter, it was quite suitable for all of the other children. Another solution was needed.

The mother said if it were just her decision, she would have kept her daughter home the day that story was reenacted. Mom would have had to come up with a pretty good explanation to give to her daughter as to why she wouldn't be attending that day.

Rev. Duughdly Durite to the rescue. The reverend talked to the girl and told her that she was specially chosen to assist the reverend that day in a very important task. The child was thrilled, and very proud, to be reverend Durite's special helper.

Lessons Learned: The mother explained the problem and offered a possible solution. The vacation Bible school organizer evaluated the proposed solution and didn't believe it could effectively be implemented. The clergy listened to the explanations and came up with an excellent solution.

The clergy's solution was a win-win for everyone. There were no demands, no whining, just an honest exchange of concerns and ideas. That's what happens in churches every day. That's the way it's supposed to be. The reverend thought *outside the box*.

A MASS FOR PEACE

Karl Jenkins wrote *The Armed Man: A Mass for Peace*. It is a delightful piece of music, which has very little to do with this vignette, other than the title.

There was a meeting of the clergy and elders. One of the elders had a personality that was quite a bit off-center. He had many good traits, but he also had some rather nonnormal traits. Well, everyone is entitled to their own character and personality traits. Life would be mighty dull if everyone thought and acted exactly the same. As a result, there would probably be little innovation, and life and culture would stagnate.

The new clergy watched and learned about his new congregation for many months. Then, at a monthly meeting with the elders, the new clergy suggested a change. Most of the elders started discussing the pros and cons of the suggestion.

One of the elders took offense to the suggestion; none of the other elders were offended. After all, it was a suggestion to be discussed and evaluated. The offended elder apparently didn't want to discuss it; he wanted to stop any discussion of the suggestion. He moved in his chair so he could get his gun. Fortunately, the other elders knew him and disarmed him.

Lessons Learned: This is a tough one. Each church, each group of elders, has to evaluate risks and solutions. Lunatics, eccentrics, and criminals are members of churches. They will always get a weapon and use it, whether it be a knife, a hatchet, a baseball bat, a gun, a ballpoint pen, or their own fists.

I've been to church services where off-duty police were hired to be in the church during every service. There were no known threats. That was just a decision of the church elders to forestall a potential threat.

In Billy Graham's book *Just as I Am,* he gives quite a few instances where he was the target of assassination or an attempt was made to shout him down.

> In Cleveland one night, police arrested three men who were attempting to get on the platform at the Invitation—one with a knife, two with pistols. (2007, page 677)

In another event, a team member saved the day.

> Team member Ralph Bell, who had been a star football player in his youth, tackled him just as he was about to reach the platform. (2007, page 677)

It's important to remember that Satan is always doing his best to mess things up. This church was fortunate to have members/elders who knew their fellow members and weren't hesitant to act.

PS: The odd elder calmed down and had a private come-to-Jesus chat with his fellow elders until he understood the error of his ways.

THANKSGIVING BREAKFAST

A friend showed me a church bulletin that gave information about the annual Thanksgiving breakfast. I'd never heard of one, but that doesn't mean they don't exist. Those who planned to attend should bring something light to share, such as fruit or pastries. The breakfast was followed by a 10:00 Thanksgiving service.

Going further in my research, I asked the senior clergy at my church. He related that was totally new to him, but he liked the idea.

I called the breakfast church and talked with the wife of the clergyman. She related that it had been an annual event at that church for years. She also related that she had been at churches that sponsored a potluck Thanksgiving dinner that was aimed at those whose families were too far away, the elderly, and the singles. Everyone came together for a joint Thanksgiving meal.

Lessons Learned: Not too much to say. It sounds like a great idea. It's something you might want to suggest to the elders at your house of worship.

SUMMARY

There are all types of personalities. Some are risk-takers; others stay with the tried-and-true. Most stay in their comfort zone but can see the options available outside their comfort zone. When necessary, they will go outside their comfort zone to try something new.

The vignettes in this chapter were about individuals who thought outside the box: the music director being an usher, the substitute for the root canal, the flexible service schedule for football, the cookie walk, and the special helper.

What is important is that when faced with an unusual situation, many comfort zone individuals will step outside their comfortable box. Quite a bit of innovation results from individuals trying something outside their comfortable box of traditional thinking. Don't be afraid to think outside the box.

— 15 —

MYSTERIOUS WAYS

Society, in general, likes to plan out events and have events follow the plan. Unfortunately, reality gets involved, and without warning, the unforeseen occurs. Some call it the proverbial bolt from the blue. Sometimes the unforeseen is something good, and sometimes, as in the "Mass for Peace" vignette, a tragedy is averted. A common phrase used for such positive events is often "The Lord works in strange and mysterious ways."

BIBLE STUDY SURPRISE

The weekly Bible study had about eight people at a table. The usual greetings were exchanged and the leader began explaining what the biblical scholars had to say about the particular verses being discussed that day.

About a quarter of the way through the hour, one of the members, whose name was Michael, said to another member, "Excuse me, what is your name?"

The other member replied, "David."

Michael said, "My name is Michael."

The two men stood up, stared at each other for a moment,

then their faces brightened. They approached each other and embraced. They hadn't seen each other for sixteen years. They were brothers.

Lessons Learned: God places people in the right place at the right time. Enough said.

THE HOUSE CALL

Ms. Gough Di Vaugh attended church on a regular basis. Then she missed several Sundays in a row. Her absence was noted by the clergy and the congregation. They thought she was ill or out of town visiting relatives.

After several weeks of absences, Ms. Gough Di Vaugh called the church office and asked the senior clergy to come see her. The clergyman thought: *She must be seriously ill. Perhaps there has been a tragedy in her extended family. The possibilities are quite extensive. It's my duty as her clergy to see her, to assist her in her time of need.*

The clergyman and his wife went to the lady's home. The clergyman and his wife thought it would probably be comforting for the poor lady to have another woman who could understand her misery—whatever that misery was.

The clergyman rang the doorbell; his wife stood to one side. That would permit the distressed lady to see it was the senior clergy coming to comfort her in her time of need.

Well, that wasn't the type of comforting the lady had in mind. She answered the door, as Lady Godiva sans her horse. The lady was stark naked! She invited the clergyman in. At that point, the wife intervened and the clergyman left with just his wife. Ms. Gough Di Vaugh remained in her home—alone—and apparently without her famous white horse.

Lessons Learned: It was quite fortunate that the clergyman was accompanied by his wife. If unaccompanied, who knows what the naked lady could have done, or would have done, when he turned her down? I'm rather sure he would have turned her down. Statically, however, I'm also sure there is a clergyman out there who might not have turned her down.

As a lady clergy told me, women and men are designed by God to have a mate. Some women (men, too) have an insatiable desire to find a suitable mate. When they don't find a mate they believe they deserve, some will employ rather unconventional methods to obtain one. Some will set out to poach a spouse from another married couple. Some will try a direct frontal approach to the problem, which Ms. Gough di Vaugh did. And some really belong in a loony bin.

Every profession has an abundance of groupies who fantasize. Some groupies are attracted to cops, athletes, film stars, or doctors—and clergy. Note that most male doctors have a female nurse present when they examine their patients, especially male doctors with female patients.

The wife of a clergy told me about a male clergy of another denomination who never works in his church alone. He said he does that to avoid the possible look of impropriety. He always leaves the church with the last staff member.

SUNDAY SCHOOL SAVED

It was a decent-sized church, and there was a children's Sunday school. During the family church service, the little ones went down the hall to the Sunday school rooms. One classroom was for children ages eight, nine, and ten.

The teacher was scheduled to arrive shortly. Well, they knew the teacher would be there shortly. But it seemed that the teacher didn't arrive—shortly, mediumly, or longly. The kids looked at each other, and a ten-year-old girl decided to lead the class. The children opened their Sunday school books to the appropriate page and class began. At the appointed time, the class ended and children returned to meet their parents.

As told to me by the ten-year-old girl, now an adult, and a clergy, the Sunday school teachers—for all grades—were recognized for their service once a year. The ten-year-old girl was recognized for her service.

PS: The ten-year-old girl's father was the senior clergy in that church.

Lessons Learned: It was fortunate that the children were well-behaved. It was also fortunate that the ten-year-old took charge of the class. What could the elders do to prevent a recurrence? Perhaps the senior Sunday school teacher should check on each of the classes at the beginning of each Sunday's session to assure that every class has an adult teacher. This is an item that each church's Sunday school program has to address. There is no one-size-fits-all solution. The prevention possibilities are numerous and will vary by denomination and individual church.

1984

The title of this vignette is the same as George Orwell's famous book. And this time, the title and the vignette do have a meaningful relationship.

Rev. Falade Moné had a healthy church. The finances were in good shape; donations and tithings were excellent. On the day of worship, the members would arrive and be seated, usually in the same seats each week.

Except on significant religious days. On those days, Rev.

Falade Moné had the ushers rope off the front four or five rows for special guests. The congregation knew who those special guests would be, the same ones who came on the last significant religious day. It would be those members of the congregation who were so busy that they were only able to attend a few times each year.

The ushers directed Mr. And Mrs. Loughtsah Douh, Mrs. Faght Chikbuk, Mr. Golde, Mr. and Mrs. Silva Mein, and others to the front rows. Now the worship service could begin. During the service, the collection plate was passed, and a second plate was usually required after the first few rows had given to the church.

After the service on significant religious days, many of the congregation would elect to leave by the side or back door of the church because Rev. Falade Moné was kept very busy by the occupants of the front rows. The congregation knew that George Orwell's principle was correct: all members of the congregation are equal, but some are more equal than others.

Lessons Learned: Rev. Falade Moné knew what was necessary to keep the church working smoothly, and so did the elders and the ushers. And apparently, so did the congregation. Could, or should, the significant religious days only attendees have been treated differently? That was a decision already reached by the elders, the congregation, and the reverend. This vignette would also have been suitable in the previous chapter, "Outside the Box," because the clergy and elders certainly thought outside the box with the affluent congregants.

As I have said previously, a lady clergyman told me one of the first things she was taught in seminary. "If it ain't broke, don't fix it."

At this church, it wasn't broke, so they didn't fix it. The elders and clergy certainly thought outside the box.

REUNION

This vignette starts in the Korean War. A young soldier, Alexander, met Kim, a Korean clergyman. Kim was a rather unusual clergy, for he spoke Korean, Russian, and Greek. Oh, and some English. Note that at one time, part of Korea had been occupied by Russia. Alexander, the American, spoke Greek, and of course, English. A bond was formed. What were the odds of a US soldier and a Korean clergyman both speaking Greek?

Fast-forward many decades. Alexander's mother dies at the age of ninety-four. Like many individuals of similar advanced age, their friends of long ago have passed. If there were not grandchildren and they were unable to attend church, the very old could have little, if any, active religious affiliation. This was the case with the ninety-four-year-old lady.

Her son found a clergy willing to do the interment service. The clergy arrived, conducted the service, and said that no one should be interred without a proper send-off. Alexander talked with the clergy afterward, and after a few minutes, the two sensed a recognition from the past. Kim, the clergy, was the same man that Alexander had met in Korea many decades ago.

Lessons Learned: God places people at the right place at the right time. The Lord works in mysterious ways.

LONG-LOST FRIENDS

Choir rehearsal, a pleasant way to end the day after a full day of work. Members come to sing, socialize, and serve their church. As with most choirs, some people move away due to their employment. Some retire and move out of the area. And of course, new members join the church or come from another church to sing in the choir with a friend or friends.

This particular evening, a new vocalist came to rehearsal. She was from another church of a different denomination. She joined this choir because she knew the music director. She introduced herself, and rehearsal began. As new pieces were being distributed, members would talk and exchange tidbits about their day.

The new lady turned around and said to a woman behind her, "I know your voice. It's very distinctive." The women exchanged where they had been during specific years. Then the light bulb turned on; they had both been military spouses in Germany fifteen years ago.

Lessons Learned: Your past will always catch up with you. And as they say, the Lord works in mysterious ways.

TWELVE MINUTES

The great virus excitement of 2020 and 2021 resulted in many people staying home. They avoided groups. They tele-churched, tele-worked, and Zoomed with friends. They self-isolated to avoid the dreaded virus that may or may not cause them harm—depending on their age and presence (or absence) of medical conditions or diseases.

Rev. Behst Shepard had an idea that would fit right in with all of the tele-thingies. The reverend instituted a Wednesday morning "Zoom-a-Prayer" program. Every Wednesday morning at 9:00, congregants could Zoom in for a short prayer session estimated to be about twelve minutes. They'd be greeted with a cheerful "Good morning." The reverend would great them by name as they logged on, and they could see the smiling face of their reverend. The reverend would say good things about life and the world, despite the dark cloud created by Satan's virus from hell.

The reverend would pray for those experiencing adversities, those with birthdays and anniversaries, etc. Each Zoomie would be thanked for joining the small Wednesday morning service. In closing, the reverend would give encouraging words and instill a feeling of optimism about life and the future. The congregants found the twelve-minute sessions a real uplifting experience.

Lessons Learned: What a way to improve, or rescue, the mental health of those isolated congregants. The "Zoom-a-Prayer" provided a weekly positive interaction, much more personal and satisfying than Sunday "Zoom-a-Church" or watching a televangelist on a TV set.

People have a need to interact with other people. The term *stir-crazy* is defined as someone neurologically affected by long, close confinement or isolation, specifically in prison.

POWs held in North Vietnam often communicated with those in nearby cells by tapping messages in code, as speaking was prohibited. The tapping reduced their isolation and helped them avoid going stir-crazy.

During the great virus experience of 2020 and 2021, a number of people began exhibiting antisocial behavior. Suicides, drive-by shootings, random hate crimes, suicides by cop, drug overdoses, and other abnormal behaviors increased. In the simplest terms, more people went bonkers. (That's a clinical term.) They stopped playing with a full deck of cards; they lost some of their marbles. A simple action that normally would be ignored became a serious slight that needed to be addressed with violence. The individual felt he, or she, had been dissed! Revenge was needed.

Sometimes when a child does something that's not acceptable, the parents interpret the action as the child "acting out." The child is seeking attention. Negative attention is better than no attention. Teachers see and recognize this in school every day.

Most hospitals have a policy requiring babies in the nursery to be picked up and held multiple times each day. Many parents soon learn that when a baby who's just been fed and had the diapers changed cries, many times the baby is really asking to be held.

When an adult acts out, the result is often violent and hurts another individual. Psychiatrists can provide lists of medical terms, explanations, and propose solutions. But as stated earlier, the individual went bonkers.

The tremendous increase in suicides and antisocial behavior can be attributed to the isolation caused by the virus pandemic. When an individual who has temporarily misplaced a few cards from his or her deck sees fame and attention given to someone by a violent antisocial act, they may conclude that that is a way to get some attention. "I'll act out and get some negative attention. After all, negative attention is better than no attention."

Too many times, the attention is posthumous.

Rev. Shephard really filled a void and deserves a great big round of applause. This clergy saw a need and took action to fill the emotional void created by Satan's virus. He thought outside the box.

USHER DUTY

There are ushers, and then there are ushers. There are good ushers, average ushers, and not-so-good ushers. And if a regular usher is inexplicably absent, a congregant will step up and fill in as usher for the service. Occasionally there are exceptional ushers.

Usher duties usually involve helping newcomers find a seat, counting the number of people in attendance, collecting the offering, etc. Duties may vary based on the denomination, the type of service, and the culture of a particular church.

In this vignette, the usher performed well outside his traditional assignment. This is about an exceptional usher.

A boy and his mother usually sat alone in the back of the church. Sensing the boy's lack of belonging, this usher asked the young lad to assist him in carrying the collection plates to the altar.

The boy beamed with pride as he accompanied the usher to the front of the church with the collection plates. *And* in future services, other members of the church started to sit beside the boy and his mother.

Lessons Learned: This usher's decision to mentor a young boy—or should I say a young man—is unique. In much of today's world, people are preoccupied with their tasks at hand. They forget, or allow, everyday courtesies to get pushed to the back of their mind. They don't consciously ignore or forget common courtesies; they just don't think about them. This usher didn't forget the common courtesies, perhaps because he was able to see the bigger picture due to his duties. He decided to reach out to the young boy and include him in the worship structure. The boy became a participant in the service, not just a member of the congregation.

This happens, with variations, in many churches. If this type of participation is not included in your particular church, it is an idea you should consider presenting. The goal is for the congregation to participate, not just observe.

SUMMARY

Some would call the vignettes in this chapter odd or rare occurrences. Another might call them serendipitous, and some might call them part of God's master plan. Psychiatrists may try to explain such events, and fortune tellers might connect them to the lines in the palms of your hands. Some clergy might say something like "It was meant to be." I lean toward the explanation that God works in strange and mysterious ways. Whatever the cause, such things happen.

— 16 —
ANTICHURCH PHILOSOPHY

Sometimes a church, or staff member, has an established procedure or policy that the vast majority of churches and clergy may find quite puzzling, perhaps even alarming. It's possible that a few readers may view one of the vignettes with the comment "What's wrong with that? My church does that, too."

In any event, I've categorized these vignettes as "Antichurch Philosophy." You can start shaking your head in frustration and disbelief now if you wish.

NOT THIS CHOIR

A mature couple was new in the area, and after settling into their home, they started looking for a church home. After rejecting one church as being too far away and another as not feeling right, they thought they had found the right church.

The church they selected had a senior clergy that seemed rather aloof to them, but they really were drawn to the assistant clergy. They saw the assistant clergy as warm and outgoing; he was very welcoming. He would walk down the aisle before the service shaking hands, greeting congregants. They described the services he conducted as a "warm worship together service."

They had decided a good way to determine if this was to be their church home was by singing in the choir. This would allow them to get a feel of the church and the congregation.

The Sunday choir was quite small for the congregation, so after church one Sunday, they asked the senior clergy about the choir. The reverend replied, "We really don't have a choir." They felt that was an odd response, but perhaps that was his assessment of the very small choir.

Not to be discouraged, they went to the choir loft and inquired about joining the choir. The small four-voice choir warmly welcomed them. Since there was not a weekday evening rehearsal, they arrived an hour early the following Sunday for the preservice rehearsal. Since they both read music, their presence was a big boost to the small choir.

There were unexpected developments during their first service with the choir. The words projected on the screens for the congregants didn't always match the words in the printed music used by the choir. This required the organist to look at the projected words and adjust—while playing the organ. That was rather demanding.

Verses 1–3 suddenly became verses 1, 2, and 4 or only verses 1 and 2. Hymn 92 was replaced with Hymn 299. Apparently, the senior clergy, Rev. Knouse Endeair, felt it necessary to adjust the verses, sometimes the words, and sometimes the hymn. The changes, however, were often made at the last minute. Sorry about that, choir.

At the end of their first service with the choir, they provided their email addresses and phone numbers. This looked like it might prove to be their new church home.

Unfortunately, the church had a bureaucracy that needed to get involved. The couple received an email several days later from the church secretary informing them that they could not join the choir until they had an interview with Rev. Knouse Endeair and formally joined the church. Only members of the church were permitted to be in the choir. The choir was a ministry and only church members could be in a ministry.

Well, the couple concluded that maybe this church wasn't for them.

Lessons Learned: A little sleuthing revealed that years ago, the church elders had instituted a policy that only members of the church who had been vetted by the senior clergy were permitted to participate in any of the church's ministries. That included the choir.

I'm sure that somewhere in that church's history, there was a reason for such a requirement. Potential members could be in the congregation and from that position decide whether to join the church.

Note: It is common for members new to a church to be asked to attend a new members class. At that class, the new members learn about the church and what the church expects of its members. Such classes and orientation are especially true for individuals new to a denomination.

I told a music director of a large church about the vetting requirement, and he said he had never heard of such a requirement. And he'd been the music director of several large churches of different denominations.

Every church is different, and some apparently have some rather unusual differences. Perhaps the elders should regularly revisit the rules that they use in guiding the church. Perhaps even explain why the vetting is necessary.

BIRTHDAY PRESENT

It was Sunday, and the senior clergy was absent. And apparently, unknown to him, an elder decided to arrange for a gigantic birthday present for him. Or should I say, an elder *said* he had decided to arrange for a gigantic birthday present for the senior clergy.

Elder Hahl Capone, seeing a great opportunity, decided to tell each family of the congregation that they were to "donate" to the church, $1,000 per family member. The funds were to provide a large birthday present for the senior clergy. That would mean a family with two parents and five children would be expected to donate $7,000 to the church. This would be in addition to any tithing.

As one would expect, most of the families couldn't afford such an expensive donation for the birthday present of the senior clergy. The result: most ignored the request and quite a few smelled something rotten, and not in Denmark or in the church kitchen but in Elder Capone. Some voted with their feet and went to another church.

Lessons Learned: First, let me assure you that this is a true vignette. The saying that truth is stranger than fiction certainly applies here. Several possible explanations for the expensive donation request come to mind.

1. Were the birthday donations really going to the senior clergy?
2. Did the senior clergy know about the donation requests?
3. Were the senior clergy and Hahl Capone running a joint Scam? Would they split some of the funds for their personal use?

4. Was Elder Capone collecting funds for his personal use? It really appears to me that it was a scam to bilk the congregants out of their money. I believe this is the most logical and likely explanation.

It's important to remember dishonest and evil people are present in all professions. Satan never takes a holiday!

NOT IN THIS CHURCH

Some people have outie belly buttons, and some have innie belly buttons. In high school, some small groups erect social walls to assure that the outies know they aren't welcome. Whether the cliques have innie or outie belly buttons is known exclusively to the clique. It's a members' only secret.

Unfortunately the clique culture hung on to one individual who brought it to "her" church. Ms. Snooty was an educated woman, a type A personality, a woman not to be crossed. Gradually, her high school clique personality began to resurrect itself. One would expect that as a senior church elder, she would be concerned with representing the entire church. Well, not if the cliquishness trait was heavily ingrained.

As time went on, she slowly assembled more responsibility and, of course, more power. And in keeping with her personality, she also started determining who would be the outies in "her" church.

Finally, some of the outies really began bumping against her innie power more and more. Didn't they realize that she was in charge, she was the innie and they were the outies? Something had to be done with those outies. Without thinking about her role as a senior elder, she elected to take power into her own hands.

An outie was having a meeting at the church one evening, the same time Ms. Snooty was having an innie meeting. The solution was obvious. She arranged for her meeting to start half an hour earlier than the outies' meeting. As soon as her meeting started, she briefly excused herself and locked the door to the church. She'd show those outies who really was at the top of the power structure. I expect Satan had a good laugh about creating a little dust-up at the church.

Unfortunately for Ms. Snooty, her childish solution was not well received by the other elders or by the congregants. The result was a come-to-Jesus meeting with the senior clergy.

Lessons Learned: Remember truth is stranger than fiction.

The other elders recognized a problem and went to the senior clergy who resolved the issue. Hopefully, Ms. Snooty will leave her immature high school cliquish behavior where it belongs—in her past. Petty issues are resolved regularly by elders and clergy at churches. That's the way it's supposed to be.

SUMMARY

Well, this chapter had some mighty unusual but true vignettes. Every organization has its own culture. In a school with five fourth-grade classes, each class has a different personality that is determined by the teacher and the students.

In a city with several churches of the same denomination, each church has a different culture based on the demographics and the clergy. Statistically, it's quite likely that one of the churches will have a culture quite different from the others. That church may even be described as a little eccentric by the other churches in the city. Until, or unless, something happens to cause a paradigm shift at the eccentric church, the culture will not change.

Rev. Knouse Endeair's need to personally approve choir

members in "Not This Choir," although probably instigated by some event in the past, stifles the church's growth. Same for Hahl Capone's donation request. Ms. Snooty's cliquish behavior was probably corrected before she caused any appreciable damage.

— 17 —

ASSORTED VIGNETTES

This chapter is an eclectic collection of vignettes and tidbits that I felt were too good to abandon. Enjoy!

THE INTERVIEW RITUAL

When a music director or assistant clergy interviews for a new position, a buzzword may be used to politely state we're not interested in you. That buzzword is *discern* or *discernment*.

The selectors tell the applicant, "We'll have to discern about that decision." That often means it ain't a gonna happen. But it's deemed polite to use those words.

It's better to just say, "We have several more candidates to interview; we'll get back to you."

The use of the word *discern* in this scenario is comparable to a young lady telling a young man that she can't go out with him on Friday night because she has to wash her hair. It's an oblique way of saying no.

It's a shame that it's not unusual that the decision has already been made regarding a new position. However, for the appearance of openness, an announcement is made, people travel for an interview, and the hiring individual or team go through the expected motions. They even go through an evaluation process when it has already been decided who is going to be hired.

ASSISTANT CLERGY INTERVIEW

A recently ordained woman applied for a position as assistant clergy at a small but growing church. She knew that the church was interviewing a number of applicants. The interview appeared to be going well. The senior clergy said that the church was always open to new ideas and welcomed everyone's ideas and opinions. The senior clergy then added, "Everyone's but yours." Needless to say, the newly ordained clergy was shocked, offended, and not hired.

The senior clergy knew the right words to say. "This church is open to new ideas." However, his controlling personality raised its ugly head. So he felt compelled to add, "Keep your ideas to yourself."

Did he feel the need to put her down because she was a woman? I talked to a friend (woman) who said she had experienced negative reactions from some men when she interviewed for a job. But she went on to add that she would rather work for a man than a woman. In her experience, many of the women supervisors were catty and cliquish.

Remember Satan is always looking for an opportunity to mess things up.

THE GREAT PIANO BENCH FIASCO

It was Easter Sunday and the reverend was delivering one of his best sermons. The congregation was paying rapt attention.

The only sound in the sanctuary was the voice of the reverend. Without warning, the music director, of above average weight, shifted his body on the piano bench. There was the unmistakable sound of splintering wood as the piano bench collapsed. All eyes were turned toward the sound. The music director slowly checked himself, stood up, and assured everyone that he was fine. After the laughter subsided, the reverend announced that since the music director was OK, he was going to continue his sermon.

PRAISE THE LORD

The choir was fully robed, their long robes almost touching the floor. The music at the moment was quite lively. The choir was standing and clapping. The choir was enthusiastic. The congregation was enthusiastic.

One of the women in the choir started experiencing an unexpected shifting of some of her clothing. She was experiencing a wardrobe malfunction! Her hosiery as coming off. What was the poor woman to do? She did the most practical thing possible; she continued singing and clapping. By the time that particular song was over, her hosiery was down around her ankles. She sat down, slipped off her shoes, shoved the liberated hosiery back under her chair, and put her feet back in her shoes.

As she reported to me, no one saw what happened, and she wasn't about to announce what had happened.

Lessons Learned: I ain't got no suggestions for this one. I forgot to ask the lady what happened to the liberated hosiery. I also failed to ask her what type of hose she was wearing, which is probably good since I wouldn't have enjoyed getting my face slapped. Did it remain for the custodian to throw in the trash? Did she go back after the service and retrieve the hosiery? If I see her again, I may cautiously ask that question.

PATH OF A CLERGY

As a teenager, Rev. Domy Bestuss was always intrigued by religion. A friend suggested he take a biblical history course while in college. He did, which he found so interesting that he entered the seminary.

Fast-forward several years. He graduated from seminary and it was time to do an internship. Fortunately, the church he attended for his internship helped him and the other new assistant work in the areas for which they were best suited or had a great interest.

Note: The individual doing the internship is often referred to as a curate or an assistant clergy (the newbie). The internship is comparable to an apprenticeship; it allows the new clergy hands-on learning in a real-life position.

Most senior clergy usually assign the newbie tasks that the senior clergy doesn't want to do (mop floors, clean toilets, etc.). The result is that most newbies leave as soon as possible, usually within a year. They seek a church where they can do what they went to seminary for or an area that they have a unique skill or interest in.

Rev. Domy Bestuss liked his first church. He and his fellow newbie decided to stay two years. At the end of two years, they had a serious talk about their future and agreed sign up for an additional five years. Rev. Domy Bestuss stayed at his first church a total of seven years. This was definitely *not* the norm. The norm is one to two years at the most for newbies.

Move time arrived. The agreed-upon five-year tour was up. What to do next? Rev. Bestuss carefully researched and submitted his résumé only to those churches that he felt were a good match for him. Once there, he implemented his get-to-know-the-church program. He had a weekly coffee session for twenty weeks, with a different group each week. After several months, he had met just about every member of the congregation. I expect there was a sign-up sheet to keep each group relatively small. He stayed at his second church for five years.

Then his last move, to a church where he has been for fourteen years—a church that uses each staff member's unique skills. Rev. Bestuss uses his best skills, as other staff members use their best and/or unique skills. The result is that his current church benefits from the wise use of each staff member. It's a situation where 2 + 2 = more than 4. The synergistic affect results in the whole being greater than the sum of the parts. That is *not* Ponzi or Bernie Madoff math.

Lessons Learned: Rev. Bestuss really lucked out at his first church in that it allowed him to discover and experience the aspect of clergy-hood that he excelled in. Yes, he can perform all the necessary clergy roles, but in a church with several clergy, he is able to perform in the area that he does the bestuss.

When the search committee or search individual is placing or hiring clergy, everyone wins when the individual's strengths match the position. This is far superior to a that'll-do or an adequate individual filling the position.

KIDDIE CHURCH

The styles and types of worship services are continually changing. The changes usually reflect what the community wants and a real or perceived void that needs to be filled. A more recent addition to some church programs is a relaxed service aimed at children. The adults can sit in the chairs or pews while the young'uns come to the front and sit on the floor or the steps to the altar.

Well, this particular church decided to check out the concept of the kiddie church program. A number of parents said they thought it was a good idea. The big evening arrived. The parents and their little ones arrived and sat together in the congregational chairs; they didn't have pews in the social hall.

After the service's opening, the little ones were invited to come to the front and sit on the floor. Rev. Child Friendly gave a simple sermon, with explanations, to her very attentive group of little ones. So far, so good. Now it was time for communion.

As she started to provide the host, the little ones thought, *Food!* All the little ones quickly rushed to the reverend to receive the nourishment. The unfortunate Rev. Child Friendly was quickly mobbed by the children seeking nourishment. The reverend had done a very good job of explaining the eucharist to them. Lots of little ones had their hands stretched out, some saying, "Me! Me! Me!" Temporarily chaos reigned. Some parents were horrified at the behavior of their children. Most of the parents laughed at the unexpected enthusiasm of their offspring. Things finally settled down and the rest of the service went off very well. After all, this was the first kiddie church service.

Lessons Learned: The relaxed kiddie service was a success—with some modifications for future services.

Henceforth, the little ones returned to the congregational seating and sat with their parents after the sermon. When it was time for communion, the children came to the altar with their mothers and fathers. The great enthusiasm of the children was now contained. Order was restored.

— 18 —

SUMMARY OF LESSONS LEARNED

Don't find fault, find a remedy—Henry Ford
I asked some friends who read the early drafts of this book for comments. As expected, comments varied. The recurring comment was for a recap of the entire book, sort of a collective lessons learned. That's what the following "sectionettes" are intended to do.

STRIVE FOR THE PERFECT CLERGY

Hiring a clergy with the intention of changing their beliefs and mores to match the church will almost always fail. And on the flip side, the clergy taking leadership of a church with the intention of changing it will almost always result in a lose-lose situation.

Explained another way, the spouse who complains the other spouse won't change is not that uncommon. In most marriages, what you see is usually what you get.

The spouse who marries him/her with the intention of

correcting the unwanted traits of their betrothed usually fails. It's the old saying about tigers not changing their stripes and leopards not changing their spots. Marrying a spouse with the intention of changing them almost always fails.

PROACTIVE COMMUNICATION

A chapter could be devoted to each vignette. One overarching missing ingredient in many of the vignettes is honest and open communication. No fingers should be crossed and placed behind one's back.

I elected not to have lengthy presentations of what-ifs and woulda-shoulda-coulda's assembled and discussed. I'll leave that to the reader to think about or discuss with friends, elders, bishop, or members of the church staff.

Honest and complete communication really helps. The old cliché "Once the cat is out of the bag, it's pretty hard to get it back in" is very true. Running a church is not a situation where "It's better to ask forgiveness than to ask for permission" is the best course of action.

HANDS-ON LEADERSHIP

Some leaders are born. Some leaders are made. And unfortunately, some individuals were born without a leadership gene. Such non-leaders are not bad people; they just should never be put in a leadership position. A five-foot, four-inch man will probably never be a basketball star. And a person with very small hands and feet will probably never be an Olympic swimmer, but they could become a great surgeon. As I stated earlier, most people have three hundred to five hundred skills they can successfully develop but only use two to four during their lifetime.

Using the magnificent tools of introspection and the rearview mirror, how many unnecessary, damaging, and painful actions could have been prevented if the responsible bishops, clergy, staff members, elders, and congregations had taken a more active and principled leadership role in the church management early on?

Dan Crenshaw, in his book *Fortitude*, stressed a number of times to avoid quick emotional responses. The news could be fake, biased, or truthful. Gather all the facts before acting. Then verify the accuracy of the facts.

NEW CHURCH, NOT A CHURCH REDO

Many of the vignettes presented were of clergy who believed it was their duty, or mission, to change the church. Rev. Super Ego views the church (the eclectic collection of ministries and congregants) as a church that needs to be changed to fit what *he* believes is the ideal church.

The three megachurches mentioned earlier (Saddleback Church, Willow Creek Church, and Church of the Resurrection) were each started by one clergy building a church from scratch. They described the *what* was *what*. The congregants knew what was being offered. They could accept or reject that church.

The unfortunate vignettes were the result of a clergy, and in the case of the "Elders Gone Wild," the elders decided what *they* wanted and took steps to achieve it. The results were damaging to the individual churches as well as to the clergy, staff, and individual congregants of the churches.

ADEQUATE IS NOT GOOD ENOUGH

As stated at the end of chapter 11, the church should not accept a mismatched clergy. It is the responsibility of the elders, the church selection committee, and/or the diocese selector to avoid making adequate or a that'll-do selection of a senior clergy. They need to think outside the box. Selectors need to regularly follow up with reviews to analyze how things went. These meetings need to be separate, and apart from, the church's regular staff meetings.

Serious consideration should be given to a probation period. Many firms have a thirty-day probation period whereby the new individual can be terminated for any reason, without recourse. Additionally, termination for unsatisfactory performance for one year. I now pose this question: why do some churches sign a multiyear contract with a new senior clergy without a probationary period? Instead, they could include a severance package in the contract to financially protect the clergy if terminated within a certain period of time—say six months.

OMBUDSMAN

Consideration could be given to a follow-up review after a few months. The church could have an independent evaluator come in and assess how things are going. I stress the word *independent*. The evaluator should not be selected by the selector or search committee. The evaluator needs to be neutral and unbiased. Perhaps a clergy from another church of a different denomination?

The review should include comments from the clergy, staff, and congregation. Determine what is going well and what is not going well. Are expectations of the clergy, expectations of the staff, and expectations of the congregation being met? Were the goalposts moved? Despite a good faith effort by all parties involved, is there a mismatch?

Perhaps a short-term ombudsman the clergy, staff, elders, and congregation could access and discuss issues with should be considered.

Suggested items that these follow-up meetings should address include the following:

* What went well with the new clergy, and why?
* What didn't go well, and why?
* Areas that the clergy believe need fixin'.
* Areas that the elders believe need fixin'.
* New ideas to be considered.
* Is the new clergy the right person for this particular church?

It is important to note that some denominations annually evaluate the clergy's suitability for the church they're serving. The clergy and the congregation are queried to determine if that particular clergy is suited, or still suited, or ill suited, for that particular congregation.

I hope that this has been a good read. If you're able to use one of the lessons learned from these vignettes, that's even better. Whenever possible, every change and every new hire should be a win-win event for the clergy, the staff, the church, the congregation, and the community. It is important to remember this: the congregation is the church.

BIBLIOGRAPHY

Christensen, Clayton M. and Taddy Hall, Karen Dillon, and David S. Duncan, *Competing against Luck: The Story of Innovation and Customer Choice*. New York, Harper Business, 2016.

Crenshaw, Dan, *Fortitude,* New York, Hachette Book Group, Inc., 2020.

Churchill, Winston S., abridgment by Denis Kelly, *Memoirs of The Second World War*. New York, Bonanza Books, 1959.

Ellison, John M. and Allix B. James, *Calling a Pastor in a Baptist Church,* Richmond, Virginia, Virginia Union University, 1966.

Entwistle, Dan, and Adam Hamilton, series editor, *Recruiting Volunteers,* Nashville, Abington Press, 2007.

Evans, Dylan, *Risk Intelligence*. New York, the Free Press, 2012.

Fisher, David, *Legends and Lies of the Civil War,* New York, Henry Hold and Company, 2017.

Graham, Billy, *Just as I Am*. New York, Harper Collins, 2007.

Hull, Raymond, *The Peter Principle*, New York, William Morrow & Company, Inc., 1969.

Janis, Irving L., *Crucial Decisions: Leadership in Policymaking and Crisis Management*, New York, the Free Press, 1989.

Lencioni, Patrick, *The Five Dysfunctions of a Team*, San Francisco, Jossey-Bass, 2012.

McRaven, William H., Admiral, USN retired, *Make Your Bed*, New York, Grand Central Publishing, New York, 2017.

Naisbitt, John, *Megatrends, Ten New Directions Transforming Our Lives*, New York, Warner Books, 1982.

Peter, Laurence J., Dr., T*he Peter Principle*, New York, William Morrow and Company, Inc., 1969.

Taleb, Nassim Nicholas, *The Black Swan: The Impact of the Highly Improbable*, New York, Random House, 2010.

Thomas, Evan, *Ike's Bluff*, New York, Little, Brown and Company, 2012.

Warren, Rick, *The Purpose-Driven Church*, Grand Rapids, Michigan, Zondervan, 1995.

Warren, Rick, *The Purpose-Driven Life*, Grand Rapids, Michigan, Zondervan, 2002.

Printed in the USA
CPSIA information can be obtained
at www.ICGtesting.com
JSHW081031190923
48555JS00001B/6